Breaking the Cycle™

A handbook to aid recovery from childhood abuse, physical abuse, sexual abuse and adversity through the C.L.E.A.N.E.R.™ Living Therapy Programme

Chris Tuck

Foreword by Emma Kenny
Media Psychologist

Published by
Filament Publishing Ltd
16 Croydon Road, Beddington, Croydon,
Surrey, CR0 4PA, United Kingdom.
Telephone +44 (0)20 8688 2598
www.filamentpublishing.com

© 2016 Chris Tuck

The right of Chris Tuck to be recognised as the author of this work has been asserted by her in accordance with the Designs and Copyright Act 1988.

ISBN 978-1-911425-24-3

Printed by IngramSpark.

This book may not be copied in any way without the prior written permission of the publishers.

In loving memory of my friend and fellow fitness professional

Cori Withell aka The Nutcracker.

I dedicate this book to Cori.

Cori was well loved and respected in the fitness industry for her expertise in mental health and nutrition.

Contents

Foreword by Emma Kenny	9
Introduction	11
My top tips to make change	23
1. Finding your deep rooted why	23
2. Speak up, speak out	24
3. Be ready for rejection	25
4. Unburden yourself	26
5. Look after yourself. Be kind to yourself	26
Surviving and thriving	28
My book, campaigning and S.O.B.	31
Why am I sharing all my achievements with you?	35
Your 7 PILLARS to Health, Wellness and Happiness!	36
Introduction to the C.L.E.A.N.E.R™ Living Therapy Programme - The 7 Pillars	38
Activities to complete and self-care	39
Grounding techniques	40
PILLAR 1 - The C.L.E.A.N.E.R™ Living Therapy Programme - CLEAR and CONSCIOUS MINDSET	41
1. Cycle of change	41
a. Acknowledge the problem	42
b. Understand the problem	42
2. How the brain develops	43
Overview of the brain	44
What the brain is made up of	44
How the brain develops	47
Long-term effects of abuse and neglect on the developing brain	50
What does a normal childhood look like? What does a normal childhood look like? NSPCC & Chris Theisen - The Parent Coach Plan	51
3. What happens when abuse/trauma occurs	52
What is abuse?	52
What is trauma?	53
Your stress response	55

The Amygdala and the Hippocampus	57
Triggers	59
How to deal with intrusive memories	60
High levels of circulating stress hormones	61
4. What can we do to help ourselves?	62
Activity 1 - 25 Smiles	62
Activity 2 - Your funeral	63
Activity 3 - The Promise/Achievement Jar	66
Activity 4 - Goal Setting	68
PILLAR 2 - The C.L.E.A.N.E.R™ Living Therapy Programme - LIFESTYLE CHOICES	75
Your average perfect day	76
Your Emotions by Nicola Mendes	83
1. Guilt	83
2. Self-blame	84
3. Shame	85
4. Anger	86
Treatments	87
1. Pharmacological treatment	87
2. Cognitive Behavioural Therapy	88
3. Counselling/Specialist Support therapies/Trauma Therapy	88
4. Meditation	89
5. Self-help groups - Peer 2 Peer Support	89
Your choices	90
Is it time for you to let go?	90
Do you have an addiction?	91
Access to help	92
Statutory Services	92
Voluntary sector (non profit) or 3rd Sector Services	94
Your responsibilities	96
PILLAR 3 - The C.L.E.A.N.E.R™ Living Therapy Programme - ENDOCRINE SYSTEM (HORMONES)	99
Endocrine System (Hormones)	99
What are hormones?	100
How do they work?	100
Cortisol	101

The Hormonal Cascade	103
Adrenal Fatigue	103
Understanding your triggers	105
Dealing with your triggers	105
Breathing	107
Eating	108
PILLAR 4 - The C.L.E.A.N.E.R™ Living Therapy Programme - ALIGNMENT (POSTURE)	**110**
Postures we adopt because of the abuse we suffered	110
The foetal position and its impact on our health	112
Signs that your posture may be affecting your health	114
What happens over time?	115
What can we do about our posture?	116
Optimum Alignment/Posture whilst standing	117
Optimum Alignment/Posture whilst Sitting	118
Optimum Alignment/Posture whilst Lying Down	118
PILLAR 5 - The C.L.E.A.N.E.R™ Living Therapy Programme - NUTRITION	**119**
What happens when we eat?	121
Water	122
Caffeine	126
Vegetables	127
Chewing	132
Digestion	134
Clean Eating v processed food and drinks	138
Wheat and Gluten	141
Dairy	143
Sugar	145
PILLAR 6 - The C.L.E.A.N.E.R™ Living Therapy Programme - EXERCISE	**149**
Exercise	149
Why is exercise so good for survivors of abuse or those living with anxiety?	150
What exercise is the best for you?	151
Getting started	152
Joining a group	153

The science of exercise and wellness	153
Over-exercise	154
Fitness online	155
PILLAR 7 - The C.L.E.A.N.E.R™ Living Therapy Programme - REST and REGENERATION	157
Sleep and the Circadian Rhythm	158
What happens if we don't get to bed early enough?	159
Stimulants and the Cortisol Cycle	160
How to improve poor sleep	161
Your plan of action	164
Coming out of survivor mode	166
Counterbalancing traumatic experiences	166
Reclaiming pleasure	167
Living in the present	169
Contact details	171
Thank you	172
Resources	174

Foreword by Emma Kenny

When I became a mother, above all I knew that I would happily take my last breath if it meant keeping my children safe. Even now, as they grow into the strong and beautiful young men that they are fast becoming, I still find myself creeping into their bedrooms whilst they sleep, just to listen to their breathing.

The privilege of being a parent, and the power invested in each and every one of us who finds ourselves blessed with a child is impossible to succinctly explain.

I only know that on a personal level, my happiness is inextricably linked to my boys and no matter where they go, this will remain a fact until I take my last breath.

I write these words with knowledge that for many children this type of parent, child relationship is a distant dream, a fantasy that will never be realised. Instead, these children wake up day in and day out with a predator so dangerous and so ever present, that they have no escape from their fear or their pain.

Sexual abuse is far more common than most of us would ever want to believe. The NSPCC recorded 57000 children who needed intervention to protect them from abuse in the home last year and this figure they suspect is eight times higher in reality.

In my therapeutic work over the last 18 years, I have been privileged to work with countless survivors of sexual abuse. Their stories have consistently angered and inspired me in equal measure. It is possible as a practitioner to distance yourself from the horror of others lived experience. I have however never mastered this in regard to child sexual abuse, I still feel the emotional jolt that courses through my body when a victim begins the process of allowing you into their terrifying world of memories that they have tried to navigate alone for far too long.

Listening to the sobs of a teenager, as they describe the terror of their childhoods is something that can never truly be prepared for. As a Mother, my instinct is to reach out to them, to hold them as they weep, but ultimately I know they need to feel their pain, and they need to create the self-safety that means they forge the resilience required to self-care for the rest of their lives. The victim must become the survivor.

I have witnessed the suffering, self sabotage, self-harm and loathing that those affected by child sexual abuse endure and without support and without understanding, this can become a life sentence of shame, that they have neither caused, nor deserve.

For me, the most powerful healing comes in the form of sharing our stories unashamedly and unapologetically. The following book is testament to that belief.

Chris is an individual who has taken the bravest step in talking about her personal experiences. This openness means that others who share her story are automatically given permission to do the same; free of the guilt and shame that silence creates.

We must learn to tell our stories, we must learn to listen to one another and we must learn that our greatest strength comes when we refuse to be tethered by the chains that others have created for us.

Emma Kenny (MBACP)

Media Psychologist/Registered Psychological Therapist

Introduction

My name is Chris Tuck.

I grew up believing that I was a nobody. For as long as I can remember I was told I was stupid, I was ugly and that nobody cared about me. I grew up to believe I was unlovable. My siblings and I suffered systematic child abuse from our stepmother (my dad was complicit by staying quiet) and later our stepfather (our mum was complicit in being abusive and staying quiet).

I was bullied by my peers at school and later on at work.

My father was convicted of paedophilia.

My sister was raped by my stepfather.

I was sexually assaulted by my stepfather.

I was groomed and sexually assaulted by a paedophile. A complete stranger, outside of the family home. I was vulnerable.

I left home when I was nearly 16.

My childhood was a desperate and lonely time. No one loved me and no one noticed how neglected I was.

I effectively became a mum to my siblings when I was seven.

In spite of all of this and more I am not just a survivor, I am thriving.

I am actively helping others, like me and you, who have found themselves in similar situations.

I do not pretend to write a book which will solve all of the child abuse trauma or mental health related issues you may suffer from. Addiction, self-harm, self-sabotage, anger issues all need the help of a trained specialist support professional such as a psychologist, psychiatrist or counsellor, a peer to peer support group may help you too.

In fact as I write these words, it's in the knowledge that I attended the funeral (last year) of an amazing woman who lost her battle with chronic depression and took her own life.

Cori Withell was 39, she was my friend and my colleague within the fitness industry working to help those who suffer from mental ill health.

Cori was supposed to collaborate with me on this book. So I can assure you I fully understand that it would be arrogant of me to claim I can fix you.

But I do believe I can help you because I understand you.

I have been there.

Years of personal and professional experience have taught me that as a survivor of abuse if you can take control back over one area of your life, like your health and fitness, it can help you towards finding the next steps in your healing journey and have a massive impact on all areas of your life.

For years I have wanted - no…..! I needed to do something to help survivors of abuse like my siblings and I. There is a real need to break the silence surrounding abuse and to help victims and survivors to reclaim their lives.

In 2012 I published a book about my life, *Through the eyes of a child*. For me, this was the start of the process. The start of my healing journey. I found my voice. I found my identity. You can download the first chapter from http://survivorsofabuse.org.uk/

My brothers Dave, Mick and my sister Diane also wrote a chapter each for the book; to show how the abuse we all suffered impacted them and their lives.

Putting my life into words and then publishing it was one of the most challenging things I've ever done. It meant digging into dark places in my heart; painful experiences and memories that I wanted to stay buried. It meant sharing with my family and my children hidden parts of my life. But publishing the book was a real turning point for me in my own healing.

By writing the book, two major things happened. One personal, the other more far reaching.

Before I wrote *Through the eyes of a child*, I didn't have a great relationship with my siblings. It was strained. We had never spoken in depth about what happened to us or how it had affected us. Throughout the writing process we gradually began to talk more. It was of course painful and caused some tension, upset and massive revelations but as we shared what happened to each of us we grew closer. My youngest sister revealed that my stepfather had raped her. My brother started to get help with managing his anger. All of this 'change' was a result of beginning to process some of the emotional damage caused by the abuse we suffered as children.

We've all started to be able to come forward and tentatively ask for help. It's one of the hardest things to do when you've been abused but it's the thing we need most. You need to feel safe, to be heard, to be believed and to trust. However, it all takes time and can be a very slow and sometimes painful process.

My brothers and sisters (I have two other sisters from my mum's second marriage) have been supportive of my efforts. My sister Diane has even stepped up to speak at events with me. Yet at the start of the process I was scared to even tell them what I was doing for fear of how they'd react.

The other thing that happened was that the more I talked openly about my experiences and the more I spoke to other survivors of abuse, the more they began to ask for help. I soon realised there was a big gap in treatment services and in advice given to those in need of help. I felt this was somewhere I could offer some advice, guidance and help.

- I am first a survivor of all forms of abuse and neglect.
- I have a thriving community based business built around health and fitness.
- I've suffered my own psychological and physical health complications caused by neglect and starvation as a child.
- I know how important it is to look after your mind and body from a nutritional, activity and de-stressing point of view.
- I am a campaigner and spokesperson for victims and survivors of child abuse.
- I have worked for and with the Priory hospital, helping them develop wellness programmes for their patients.
- I have created the Breaking the Cycle™ C.L.E.A.N.E.R.™ Living Therapy Programme to help victims and survivors to start to heal where ever they are on their journey.

I am confident that if you can take control of your health - your mental, emotional and physical health, through mindset, education, nutrition, fitness and de-stressing your body, you will also be in a better place to want help with the bigger, deep rooted stuff that is affecting you.

I'm not talking about a radical, unachievable overhaul here. I'm talking about simple changes.

And this book isn't just for survivors of abuse, child abuse or domestic violence. Yes, that's my starting point and yes, this is where I feel I can help the most but the strategies which help survivors are the same strategies which can help anyone suffering with mental health issues like chronic anxiety, depression or PTSD that are not related to abuse. The starting points might be different but the effects on the body are similar.

Suffering from mental health illness can result in a cycle of self-harm. Be it negative mind talk, low self-worth, disordered eating or addiction/substance abuse and that cycle can only be broken by you.

This programme has been devised to make it simple to follow and achievable. These are all steps which you could do without guidance if you wanted to but where my book is different is that I'm laying it all out for you as a step by step process. I understand the challenges you face because I have been there myself and continue to work on my challenges every day.

You deserve help. You deserve to feel 100% healthy and 100% happy, to live your life to your full potential.

Breaking the Cycle™ is literally that. It's about taking a fresh look at how you feel, what you eat, what exercise you do, and your lifestyle behaviours. It's about challenging the way you 'look after' yourself. It's about tweaking your lifestyle to begin to break your self-harm cycle. Be it mental or physical.

I want you to know that I fully understand how difficult this is. Constantly telling yourself you are not worth looking after IS NOT GOOD FOR YOU. I know this. You know this. But if it were that easy to make a change there wouldn't be thousands of men and women currently in these cycles of negative behaviour.

Can you relate to any of the following?

- Self harm;
- Addiction to alcohol, drugs or food;
- Depression;
- Anxiety or fear;
- Low self-worth or lack of self-esteem;
- Post Traumatic Stress Disorder (PTSD), or
- Suicidal tendencies.

Are your thoughts and feelings all over the place that you can't lead a normal life?

These are all ways of 'coping' with your emotions when you cannot say what is happening to you or when you can't process your feelings.

I know that getting the right help when you need it is not easy. Waiting lists for specialist support services (talking therapies) are oversubscribed/underfunded and there's a long waiting list even if you can afford to pay for private therapy.

I feel that I can help you cope better with your challenges by sharing what has worked for me and others.

So Breaking the Cycle™ is about empowering you to take some power and control back over your life. I want to teach you how you can make changes; how you can begin to break the cycle. And I want to support you through the process.

My focus for you is YOUR health and well-being. As I've said before, I'm not a psychologist or a doctor. I can't prescribe medication (certainly not through the pages of a book) but I can be here for you. I can show you what helped me deal with the impact of the abuse I suffered.

As my friend and fitness colleague Cori Withell always said: "Your food choices will affect your mood and your mood will affect your food choices."

If you can boost your mood, you might not need a prescription for anti-depressants. Don't believe me? I work with clients every day who no longer need anti-depressants because of the positive food choices and activity changes they have made in their lives.

I work with fitness and health professionals every day whose clients no longer need anti-depressants because of the positive diet and activity changes they have also made in their lives.

I no longer need anti-depressants because of the positive diet and activity changes I've made in my life.

Have I made my point?

Taking back power and control can make you feel better about yourself. It can begin to stop the negative mind talk. It will make you feel empowered.

Breaking the Cycle™ is already having a positive impact on people's lives.

Here are just some of the changes my Breaking the Cycle™ participants have already noticed:

- Moods more stable.
- Fewer bouts of depression and/or anxiety.
- Less pain and inflammation.
- Decrease in blood pressure.
- Decrease in cholesterol.
- Blood sugar stabilised.
- Improved self-esteem and self-worth.
- Increased energy/more alert.
- Increased ability/desire to take responsibility for self.
- Improved frame of mind.
- Improved sleep patterns

In short, Participants are moving from a place of surviving to thriving. Something I want for all of you.

Here is a testimonial from one of S.O.B's current clients:-

Chris has shown me that there really is light at the end of the "dark and desperate tunnel"! It's such a relief to be under her expert guidance. I really look forward to her inspirational sessions because I'm making great progress in her safe hands. After years of being in the doldrums through knee injuries and operations I'm now much fitter, healthier and much more confident.

Having recovered from hip operations herself, Chris's personal insight into managing pain and avoiding further injury has been invaluable. She ensures that each new exercise is paced at just the right level. The following session she always listens very carefully to my feedback to see how my body reacted afterwards. I'm delighted that my knees are much stronger and that my range of movements and stamina has vastly improved.

Chris's wealth of experience is reflected in her enthusiastic advice about the right combination of fitness and nutrition. The Breaking the Cycle™ C.L.E.A.N.E.R.™ Living Therapy Programme has been so effective. It's much easier to follow than I thought because you can eat delicious healthy meals without having to weigh everything or going hungry. I was genuinely surprised that I don't need to graze in between meals anymore. Also surprised how easily the inches and pounds slipped away and how the knee pain has disappeared.

Because I feared injury and another operation I reluctantly gave up tennis and dance years ago. I've been desperate to get back to fitness but hadn't been able to find the right PT or fitness class instructor who I felt would understand the sensitive highs and lows. However, thankfully, I came across Chris and her first book called Through the eyes of a child just a few weeks ago.

Although our circumstances have been completely different, her account of trying endless ways to recover from the impact of child abuse resonated with me as a fellow survivor. Despite always looking cheerful on the outside I had become fearful of triggers from close contact with professionals and people in certain situations.

Chris completely understands the complexity of this dilemma. She listens and encourages with great empathy. Each supportive session builds towards achievable goals. Chris is such a sensitive and motivational teacher and I've already recommended her to many different people. I've enjoyed a staggering turnaround, not only in my in my fitness but in my mental health growth. My family are so thrilled and proud.

(Name Anon)

Let's go back a little... I'd like to share with you what it feels like for me when I get triggered and what happens to me mentally and physiologically (how my mind and body respond to my triggers).

Let me set the scene by starting with a short synopsis of my life:-

In the first 16 years of my life I moved home at least eight times and moved families twice.

At one point in that childhood I lived in a tent in Wales for six months, during winter because my dad and step mum evaded rent payments.

I ended up in the local homeless unit three times.

I moved schools frequently and sometimes didn't go to school.

My siblings and I were malnourished, beaten and neglected by our caregivers (parents).

We were of course also bullied at school for our appearance, behaviour and for being different.

My childhood was the pits. It was emotionally and physically damaging, especially for my siblings. I became the mum to my two brothers and one sister.

When you have experienced one or a series of traumatic events this can be a major stress on your mind and body and if your thoughts and feelings have not been processed properly you can be triggered at any time by flashbacks, intrusive memories, nightmares and panic attacks.

WARNING the following description maybe upsetting for some of you.

This is what happened to me when I get triggered sometimes.

Thump. Thump. Thump.

My heart is banging in my chest.

I feel like my heart might explode.

I can feel the blood pumping in my ears.

My breathing becomes shallow and fast.

My muscles get tight.

My pupils dilate.

My body is fully alert and ready.

I'm scared. I'm anxious. All of my senses are heightened.

I can smell, touch, taste, feel and see exactly what is going to happen. AGAIN.

I've been here hundreds of times before.

Here comes my abuser.

I'm ready to do whatever it takes to survive.

I might run away. I might freeze and just take what's coming. Or today I just might stand my ground and fight.

Is this a real event? Is this a memory? Is this my nightmare?

It doesn't matter. The brain when you suffer/experience trauma sees it as all the same thing. It's a threat to my survival.

Even when the threat is not a physical one anymore, my body prepares itself to fight, or to run, or to freeze. Every time. It's like a broken record that is stuck.

My emotions and feelings have become hard wired in my brain. Unless I deal with the real cause of the 'threat' every little threat can make me react in the same way. I will constantly be frightened of my own shadow, living in fear. Not living the life I deserve.

For many abused people this is a constant cycle, it's their reality. What's actually happening is that we live in constant fight/flight mode. Our bodies are in a constant state of heightened stress. And for people suffering from chronic anxiety or depression it can feel much the same way.

I will explain the science behind being triggered by flashbacks, intrusive thoughts and nightmares later in the book and how you can deal with them.

After the threat passes my body slumps.

I am tired.

My body craves carbohydrates.

I am now in a cycle of emotional eating. A cycle many abused people will be familiar with.

I crave sweets, chocolate and cake. Anything that will make me feel good for a moment. Anything to fill the void. There's now a big black hole in my stomach and in my head which I try to fill with food (you may have different coping strategies)

Then the guilt starts. I berate myself. I gain weight. I feel fat. I feel unloved and unworthy. My self-esteem hits rock bottom. I feel under threat and the cycle continues. I reach for more comfort food.

I developed bulimia as a way of coping with episodes in my life where I was experiencing high levels of stress. It's was my way of coping.

This is my cycle of threat and disordered eating. The bulimia is a reactionary behaviour. It's a response to what my body sees as an immediate threat, even though it's in my head, my body responds physically, but unconsciously.

Other survivors of abuse turn to alcohol, drugs, self-harm, anorexia, disordered eating, fighting, crime, sleeping around (mistaking sex for love).

All survivors of abuse and many who suffer with chronic anxiety or depression will be very familiar with these cycles. But over time, these reactionary behaviours become habitual.

It's at this point that they begin to harm your mental, physical and emotional well-being. When disordered eating or addictions become habitual behaviours we need an external influence to help 'break the cycle'. We need access to specialist support services.

In 2000 I had a breakdown and the only way I could turn my life around was to 'break the cycle' of what I was doing to myself. I knew it was time to acknowledge I had a problem. I needed to understand what was happening to me and I needed a solution to my problem. None of this is easy when you don't trust anyone, when you are ashamed of who you are, what you do and when you are afraid of what will happen if you do tell someone.

But deep down it was obvious I needed to make some changes in my life if I was ever to be mentally and physically well.

But I didn't know what to do or where to begin!

Until I took the first step...

My top tips to make change

Any change is scary. It can feel much more comfortable to stay as you are. Even if what you know is abuse and misery. This is especially true when you believe that your abuse is normal or that you deserve it. When you've never known anything different, or perhaps your self-abuse has become so habitual that you've forgotten a different way of living.

These five top tips have helped me move on from the abuse I suffered and are still helping me.

1. Finding your deep rooted why

You need to be feeling enough discomfort (pain) to first seek change and to ensure your success. It will help you through dark times or tough times. It will make you commit to the change.

When I was 15 I knew I had to leave home. For me there was no other option. I had no money. I had nowhere to live. I wanted to go to college but I was only 15 nearly 16. In spite of the challenges in front of me I was so miserable at home that for me, getting out was the only option. I was so angry and I felt so trapped that I feared I would erupt and cause my 'caregivers' / abuser - serious harm.

- I had to leave the childhood abuse I suffered behind.
- I wanted more for my life.
- I wanted something different.
- I wanted to be loved.
- I wanted to be happy and healthy.
- I believed this was only possible if I left home.
- I wanted security.

- I craved stability and a family of my own.

All of the above drove me to succeed to fulfil everything that I set out to achieve.

Don't get me wrong I was so scared about the change ahead of me, I didn't want to leave my siblings but I felt that my back was up against the wall and that I had no other option.

As I got older my aims and goals changed slightly but the need for security and stability never wavered and this drove me on through many years of studying and failing!

2. Speak up, speak out

Find someone you trust to talk to. It might be a friend, a family member, a stranger or a colleague who you can trust. If you don't have someone in your family or friendship circle you can confide in then consider a Peer 2 Peer support group like S.O.B Breaking the Cycle™ or Shatterboys UK, or call one of the many helplines that are available via the NSPCC, NAPAC, the Samaritans, the Survivors Trust or Rape Crisis.

Do not think that you are alone.

There are many people in the world who have been abused.

According to the NSPCC 1 in every 20 people have suffered from some kind of abuse and 50,000+ children in the UK are in need of child protection.

In November 2015, the children's commissioner, Anne Longfield, in her Nov 2015 report, Protecting Children from Harm (http://www.childrenscommissioner.gov.uk/learn-more/child-sexual-exploitation-abuse/protecting-children-harm), stated:

"Only one in eight children are known to have reported the abuse they suffered as a child".

This means that only one in eight received the vital intervention needed to keep them safe and help them to overcome their experiences.

It also means that seven out of eight children are growing up as adults whose lives will be impacted in some way - be it through addictions, depression and anxiety, PTSD, relationship issues or other problems, as a result of the abuse they have suffered.

So you can clearly see you are not on your own. And no matter how bad you think your situation is; how ashamed you feel or how much you have been silenced by the abuser I believe you must speak up and speak out for the sake of your own mental and physical well-being. My reasons for saying this will become clear as you work through the book.

Take the first step in freeing yourself from the abuser(s). Say NO to the abuser(s) and tell someone you trust about the abuse in confidence or go straight to the Police if you want to pursue the abuser(s) through the criminal justice system.

3. Be ready for rejection

Things will not always go to plan. Your journey towards freedom from self-sabotage will, of course, be littered with hiccups.

Believe in yourself and be ready to see your plan through regardless of setbacks. Expecting them means you are already insured against failure.

Life can be harsh and when you finally find the courage to speak up and speak out you may not be believed. If this does happen to you it isn't your fault. The person you have spoken with may not be ready to hear the truth. They may never be ready. Contact one of the organisations listed above or in the back of this book. They can help you to move forwards and get the help that you need and deserve.

4. Unburden yourself

Let go of the abuse you suffered and your stress by taking the action necessary for you to lead a happy and healthy life. This is your right as a human being. After my breakdown in 2000 I had therapy to help me get through my childhood trauma. I was scared. I felt ashamed. I felt guilty. I was full of anger and resentment. All of which was making me unwell. Both mentally and physically.

You may resent having to spend time working on actions to help you move forwards.

Perhaps even reading this book is inducing guilt. But you deserve to be happy and unburdened from the person(s) who abused you.

5. Look after yourself. Be kind to yourself

- Learn to de-stress your body.
- Eat nutritious food.
- Choose an activity or exercise that you enjoy and
- Take time out for you.

I will go through the four points above in great detail but this is the essence of the Breaking the Cycle™ C.L.E.A.N.E.R.™ Living Therapy Programme.

To help me understand the abuse I suffered I read many books, listened to other stories, had therapy and wrote my book.

I took small, positive steps in the right direction. At times it was challenging but I was focused on my goal and going back was never an option. I built up my confidence and went after what I wanted. I wanted to help other people like us escape from abusive childhoods. Part of me knew that unless I moved on from my own challenges - I could never help others.

I have achieved my goals through maintaining a positive mindset, de-stressing, eating right for me and getting the right activities and exercise into my life.

I believe that you can achieve anything you want to and with the help of people like me and my siblings who are openly talking about the damage of decades of abuse, YOU can move forwards with your life too.

Now is the time to take the first step. It may feel like there's such a tough road ahead that you can't face the first step but right now, the first step is all you need to take.

I have two sayings that I live by:

>If nothing changes, nothing changes.
>
>and
>
>Be true to yourself.

Let's start this journey together wherever you are on yours.

Surviving and thriving

What does it mean to move from a position of surviving to thriving? It means you no longer just cope.

It means you no longer just survive day to day with a smile pasted on to your face.

It means you find coping mechanisms and outlets for your 'issues' which are positive and not harmful to you or others.

It means making something of your life, regardless of your emotional (or sometimes physical) scars.

For many survivors of abuse it means making something of your life because of your scars and the adversity that you have endured.

It means living out your life to the potential you always dreamed of - rising from the tangled mess into something whole and full of fire.

To me it means much more than plodding along in life. Some people want an easy life but I just don't think it's in me to play it safe.

When you're abused as a child, your view of the world is completely messed up. As an abused child, your aspirations and dreams are very different to what non-abused children dream of.

As a child, all I wanted was food and parents who loved me. I wanted to be a child. I craved stability and security. So my aspiration was to get a job and a secure roof over my head with food in my cupboards.

But now I'm through with the surviving stage. I'm thriving.

From the age of 0-7 I don't remember my life. There are only a handful of photos of this time in my life. My mum left when I was 7 because she said my dad hit her and had affairs and she couldn't take it anymore. My siblings and I were brought up in a domestic violence household.

From the age of 7-11 I just survived. This was the most miserable part of my life with my dad and stepmum.

From the age of 11-15 I survived but the abuse continued with my mum and stepdad.

From the age of 15-28 I left home and started to build my own life - I both survived and thrived using coping strategies to get me through. I 'ran away' from my past. I shut it away and tried to forget about it. I never talked about what happened to anyone. I didn't want anyone to judge me in any way.

At the age of 28 I had my son and my mental health began to slide

At the age of 30 I had a breakdown/breakthrough. At the time it felt like my life was falling apart and that I would never recover. Everything I had built for myself and my family, my reputation, my health and wellness could have been lost. But looking back, this was the time that I truly see as my 'breakthrough'. Reconciling the past to be able to truly be at peace with who I was and to regain the authentic me.

From the age of 30-42 I was getting to grips with what happened to me as a child. My own inner child came out of the shadows and wanted to be heard, cuddled, loved, nurtured, cared for. She wanted to scream and shout. Both my mental health and physical health was impacted but this was also the start of my healing journey.

At the age of 42 I wrote and released my book *Through the eyes of a child* with the help of Karen Laing, my ghost writer.

From 42 to NOW, 2016, I am mainly thriving but my family has just reported the abuse we suffered as children to the Police so this is now triggering me and causing great pain and anxiety at times. At these times I am just surviving! But I know I will get though this and then will be able to use my experience to help others.

Don't get me wrong, life isn't perfect. But I'm able to use what I know and my past experiences to help others, like us. I'm able to give something back to the world.

The abuse I suffered no longer belongs to me. It is no longer shameful. It's almost as if the abuse happened to someone else. The more I share and the more I talk, the more powerful I become, and the more the abuse and the abuser loses power and control.

The abuse no longer has a hold over me. It no longer frightens me.

You may have noticed that I don't say 'MY' abuse - I say 'the' abuse. I don't say 'MY abuser' - I say 'the abuser'.

When we use the term 'MY' it implies that it belongs to us, that we are responsible for something!!!

We are NOT responsible for the abuse that we suffered; the abuser doesn't belong to me. I didn't want the abuse to happen to me nor did you.

Let's put all the associated feelings - the shame, the blame, the guilt back at the abusers door.

I don't want it, I don't deserve that - nor do you!!!

For me, thriving is about hitting the campaign trail and helping other victims and survivors of child abuse. Past, present and sadly, future.

Writing my book was just the beginning. Becoming a Health Coach and understanding the impact of the abuse I suffered on both my mental and physical health has now given birth to the charity Survivors of Abuse. - S.O.B. I knew I needed to do more to help victims and survivors. …. and not just a few of us….lots as many of us as possible.

Writing and publishing *Through the eyes of a child* has both empowered and emboldened me.

My book, campaigning and S.O.B.

When I first met with my ghost writer, Karen, back in 2012, I was afraid to share everything.

As we wrote the book, together, I was gradually able to reveal more about what had happened to me. I went into the loft gathering hordes of notebooks that I'd written details in. All failed attempts to get my story onto paper. It was too emotive for me.

Back in March 2012 I hadn't even spoken with my siblings about everything that had happened to me. We weren't really talking. But the more I wrote my memories; the good, the bad and the ugly came back full force.

Eventually my siblings and stepsisters shared everything that had happened to them too.

My sisters who had to sleep with their knickers on; for fear of the stepfather.

My brother had to get help with his anger management before it tore his family apart.

My sister had been sexually abused and raped by the stepfather. It all came out.

I've seen so much of what really happens to abused children:-

- The 'safe' houses.
- The system.
- The teachers that don't see.
- The bullied children who become bullies.
- The time I spent at the local children's home.
- The way that abused children are vulnerable to paedophiles and abuse from outside of the home, especially if that child runs away and lives on the streets.

- The trouble that abused children get into because they are so angry, many becoming addicts getting into trouble with the law.

- The lack of adequate mental health provision and specialist support services for adult victims and survivors of childhood abuse.

I know exactly how it feels to be an abused child who no-one believes.

I know exactly how it feels to have no-one to turn too.

Child abuse does not end with the abuser and the abused child. Family relationships are destroyed, lives are destroyed, and abuse causes both mental and physical health challenges to all caught up in its web.

And so as momentum grew I knew I had to do something more than just paint on a smile and sign books.

Through my book and through the charity Survivors of Abuse (S.O.B) I am now doing everything I can to push child abuse to the top of the agenda and make politicians, media outlets and society as a whole understand what it's really like.

But can they even begin to understand how it feels?

Survivors of Abuse (S.O.B) was granted charity status in April 2016 and funds from the book sales are going directly to S.O.B to help others who need support to live their lives.

I've been interviewed by Eamonn Holmes on Sky TV. The first time following the Rotherham Scandal and again following revelations of 11 million victims of child sexual abuse in the UK. And finally following the Lambeth scandal.

11 million. You are absolutely not alone.

I've also been interviewed by the BBC for a documentary, *The Scale of Abuse*.

I've appeared in the *Daily Mail*, the *Guardian* and the *Sunday Mirror*.

I've been in my local news and on talk shows with Pauline Long and Chrissie B. And I have worked with the broadcaster and national ambassador for Domestic Abuse UK, Jenni Steele who is now a close friend.

If you're a victim or a survivor of child abuse, you will know exactly how hard it is to expose yourself to anyone let alone national media. To share the abuse you have suffered to share your story.

That thing that you try to bury inside yourself.

It was the same for me but I've learned to use my experiences to help others, like us because this is what I feel is of utmost importance.

To break the silence and to break the cycle.

I have been involved in the focus groups for the Children's Commissioner Inquiry into child sexual abuse within the family environment.

In November 2014 I first met with Theresa May along with many other survivors at the Home Office to see how we could help with the Inquiry. I've since met with many other amazing victims and survivors of abuse who all have their own stories and experiences to share and I have gained great insight and an understanding to the true scale of the problem we face with child abuse in England and Wales.

It is truly an epidemic in fact it is endemic in our society; like a cancer silently creeping through and no one wants to talk about it.

Networking - As part of my campaign to get better services for adult victims and survivors of non recent child abuse I have met with people like Pete Saunders the founder of NAPAC, Tom Rail CEO from the Priory, Colonel Bob Steward MP - my local MP, celebrity Linda Robson, Eamonn Holmes from Sky News, and Emma Kenny, TV psychologist, presenter, writer and expert commentator.

These people haven't approached me. I've created connections through networking. Face to face and via social media. I have no special PR person or advisor working for me. This is all little me, getting out there and throwing it back at the people who abused me. This is the scariest thing I have ever done reaching out to strangers!

They tried to keep me down but I'm rising. So can you!

Public speaking - I've taken my story into schools and colleges. At first sharing advice on nutrition, motivation and fitness and then using my story to talk about bullying and the importance of education.

I have spoken at Universities to undergraduates and postgraduate students in social care and have presented to professionals at RASASC in Guildford, and East to West about my life to raise awareness of the impact of childhood abuse on the child, adolescent and the adult.

I have spoken in Parliament twice.

In September 2014 I hosted the first ever Breaking the Cycle™ Life After Abuse Conference in central London.

In May 2015 I hosted the first ever Breaking the Cycle™ retreat and I co-directed the first Breaking the Cycle™ Child Abuse Rally in central London in 2015 with Chris Wittiwer.

In July 2015 I joined the VSCP as a consultant to IICSA, the Independent Inquiry into Child Sexual Abuse.

I host a weekly Facebook live conversation on Sundays at 7.30pm where we discuss anything to do with child abuse, its impact and how we recover.

#LifeAfterAbuse   #BreakingTheCycle   #SOB

Why am I sharing all my achievements with you?

I am no different to you. You might be thinking, 'I couldn't do that.' But I've been in your shoes.

I have just become used to stepping out of my comfort zone because I'm so impassioned about helping people like us.

It's what drives me to get up in the morning and to make a difference every day!

Celebrating our achievements is all part of rebuilding our self-esteem and our recovery to fulfilling our potential, reclaiming ourselves and restoring our health and wellness.

Before we can start looking at the 7 PILLARs of the Breaking the Cycle™ C.L.E.A.N.E.R.™ Living Therapy Programme (created by Chris Tuck from http://www.survivorsofabuse.org.uk), we need to acknowledge the impact of childhood abuse on us as individuals.

There is a lot of research out there to show and validate the impact of child abuse but the most compelling piece of research that I have been notified of is the ACE Report - Adverse Childhood Experiences (https://www.cdc.gov/violenceprevention/acestudy/).

'Childhood experiences, both positive and negative, have a tremendous impact on future violence victimization and perpetration, and lifelong health and opportunity. As such, early experiences are an important public health issue. Much of the foundational research in this area has been referred to as Adverse Childhood Experiences (ACEs).

ACEs can be prevented.

Learn more about preventing ACEs in your community.'

Your 7 PILLARS to Health, Wellness and Happiness!

As a result of the impact of the childhood abuse I suffered on my mental, emotional and physical health and recovery I created the Breaking the Cycle™ C.L.E.A.N.E.R.™ Living Therapy Programme.

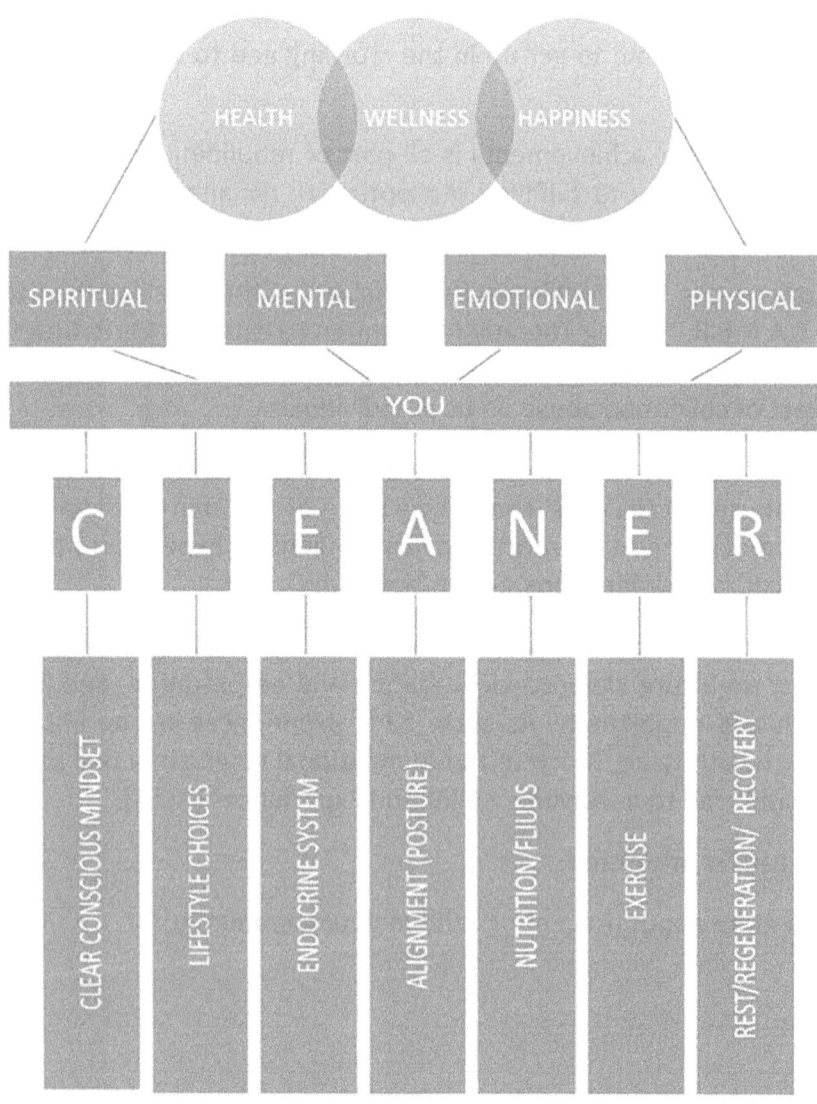

There are 7 Pillars to the Breaking the Cycle™ C.L.E.A.N.E.R.™ Living Therapy Programme which form the foundations of your health and wellness. The PILLARs interconnect and interrelate and work in synergy.

When you are successfully implementing all the Pillars into your everyday life you will experience optimum mental, emotional and physical health.

When one Pillar is not working effectively it will impact on all of the other Pillars and this will affect YOU, your mental, emotional, physical health and wellness and ultimately your happiness.

And conversely when you're mental, emotional, physical health and wellness is not good this will impact YOU from implementing all the Pillars successfully.

The 7 Pillars are the foundations to your health, wellness and happiness.

You will clearly see the interrelationships between the PILLARS as you work through the book. You may think you are reading the same thing twice! This is not a mistake but clearly shows you the how important it is to think about your mind and body as one entity rather than separate entities and how you can make a massive change to your health, wellness and happiness through the ripple effect of taking one small step, then two small steps and so on.

Right it's time to have a look at the 7 Pillars in more detail!

Pillar 1 - Clear & Conscious Mindset

Pillar 2 - Lifestyle Choices

Pillar 3 - Endocrine System

Pillar 4 - Alignment

Pillar 5 - Nutrition

Pillar 6 - Exercise

Pillar 7 - Rest & Regeneration

Introduction to the C.L.E.A.N.E.R™ Living Therapy Programme - The 7 Pillars

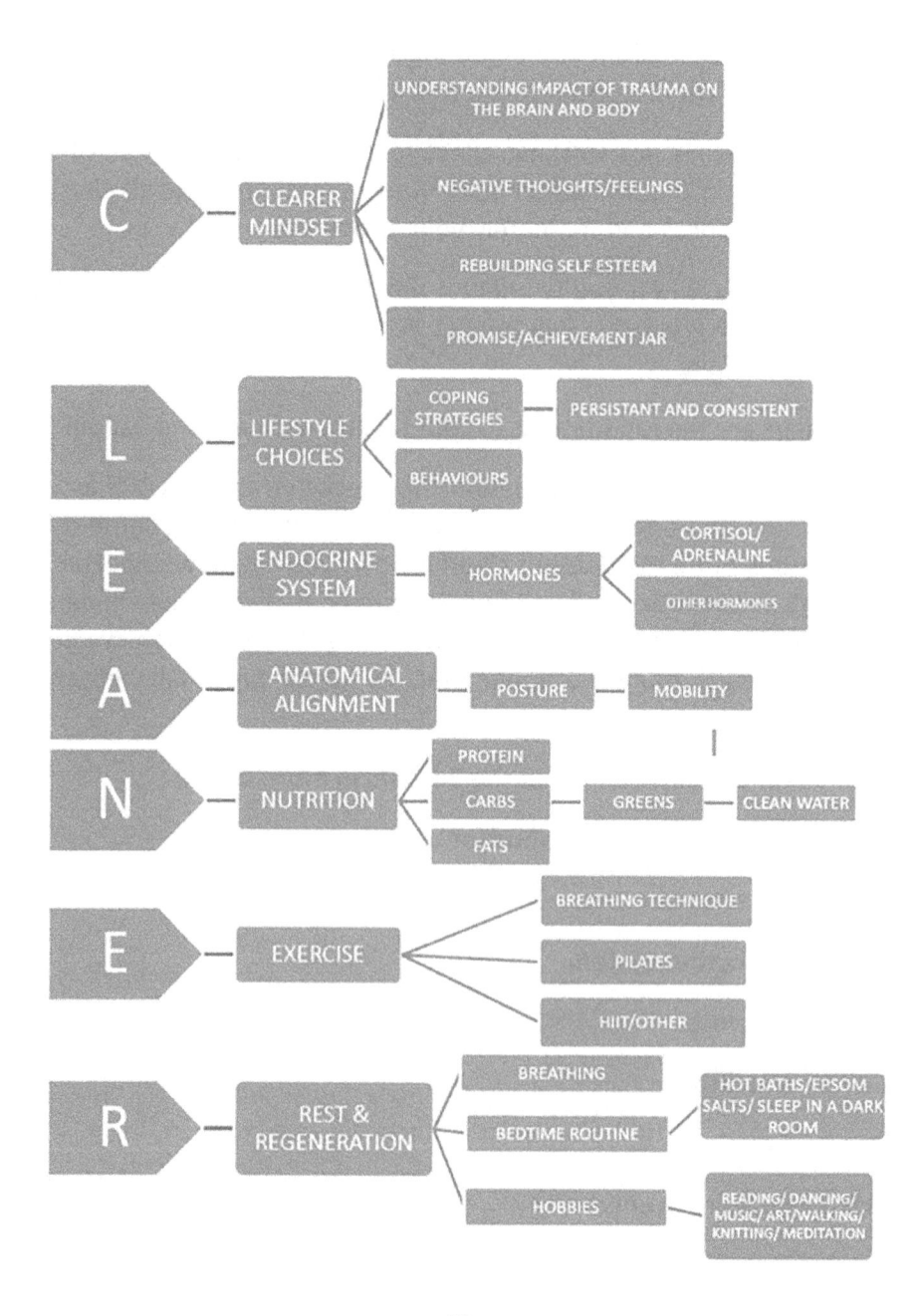

C — CLEARER MINDSET
- UNDERSTANDING IMPACT OF TRAUMA ON THE BRAIN AND BODY
- NEGATIVE THOUGHTS/FEELINGS
- REBUILDING SELF ESTEEM
- PROMISE/ACHIEVEMENT JAR

L — LIFESTYLE CHOICES
- COPING STRATEGIES — PERSISTANT AND CONSISTENT
- BEHAVIOURS

E — ENDOCRINE SYSTEM
- HORMONES
  - CORTISOL/ADRENALINE
  - OTHER HORMONES

A — ANATOMICAL ALIGNMENT
- POSTURE — MOBILITY

N — NUTRITION
- PROTEIN
- CARBS — GREENS — CLEAN WATER
- FATS

E — EXERCISE
- BREATHING TECHNIQUE
- PILATES
- HIIT/OTHER

R — REST & REGENERATION
- BREATHING
- BEDTIME ROUTINE — HOT BATHS/EPSOM SALTS/ SLEEP IN A DARK ROOM
- HOBBIES — READING/ DANCING/ MUSIC/ ART/WALKING/ KNITTING/ MEDITATION

Activities to complete and self-care

Under some of the PILLARS there are some activities for you to take part in.

Please only complete the activities that you feel that you can cope with at this moment in time.

You can always skip activities and come back to them at a later date if you choose too!

Grounding techniques

If you become upset at all throughout this book please practice self care.

Use your grounding techniques to bring yourself back to 'normal'.

- Practice your belly breathing
- Recall your safe space
- Practice the Hear and Now technique
- Call a friend or a helpline listed in the back of the book
- Talk to us in the Breaking the Cycle™ secret Facebook group.

PILLAR 1 - The C.L.E.A.N.E.R™ Living Therapy Programme - CLEAR and CONSCIOUS MINDSET

Under this Pillar we are looking at a clear and conscious mindset and its impact on both our mental and physical health. Clear and conscious means being fully aware of and being in charge of the decisions you are making.

We need to look at and understand how child abuse affects us. To explore this we will be looking at the following:-

1. The Cycle Of Change
2. How The Brain Develops
3. What Happens When Trauma/Abuse Occurs
4. What We Can Do To Help Ourselves

- Activity 1 - 25 Smiles Activity
- Activity 2 - Your Funeral Activity
- Activity 3 - The Promise / Achievement Jar Activity
- Activity 4 - Goal Setting

1. Cycle of change

a. To find solutions to any problem we need to acknowledge that a problem exists

b. We need to understand the problem

c. We need to find solutions to solve the problem

d. We need to act on these solutions

We need to continually assess if the solutions are working and take more action if needed

a. **Acknowledge the problem** - what are your symptoms?

- Self Harm
- Addiction - Alcohol / Drugs / Food
- Depression
- Anxiety / Fear
- Low self worth / lack of self esteem
- PTSD / DID
- Suicidal Tendencies
- Are your thoughts and feelings all over the place to such extent that you cannot lead a normal life?

b. **Understand the problem**

- Why are we suffering from these symptoms?
- Why are these symptoms preventing us from living a normal everyday life?
- Why can we not 'just' get over the symptoms and get on with life like everyone expects us to?

These are our coping mechanisms for dealing with trauma/childhood abuse

Liz Mulliner Research into Mental Health Australia 2005 (https://www.youtube.com/watch?v=svX3fEdVTLQ) showed that

- 69.9% of psychiatric inpatients
- 82-86% Bipolar disorders
- 90% Personality disorders

- 80% depression/anxiety

suffered from Childhood Trauma.

From these statistics (and it has only gotten worse in England and Wales with people coming forward and disclosing) it's clear that child abuse impacts many of the Mental Health conditions. We know child abuse is prevalent; we already know that it has a massive impact on the victim and survivor's mental, physical wellness and quality of life. We need to urgently look at and develop clear care pathway(s) to offer victims and survivors so that they can recover from child hood trauma.

To understand why victims/survivors suffer from mental health and physical health conditions we need to look at how our brain develops.

2. How the brain develops

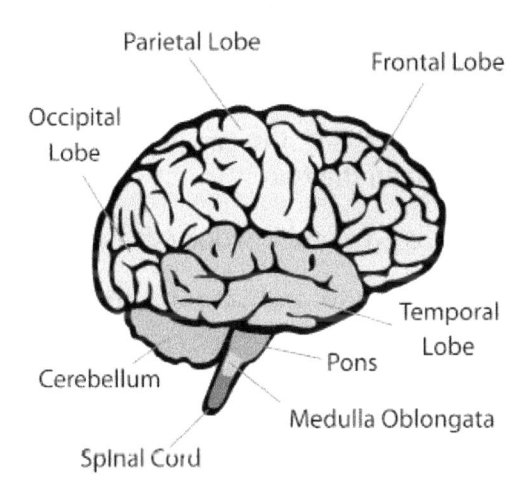

LIMBIC SYSTEM STRUCTURES

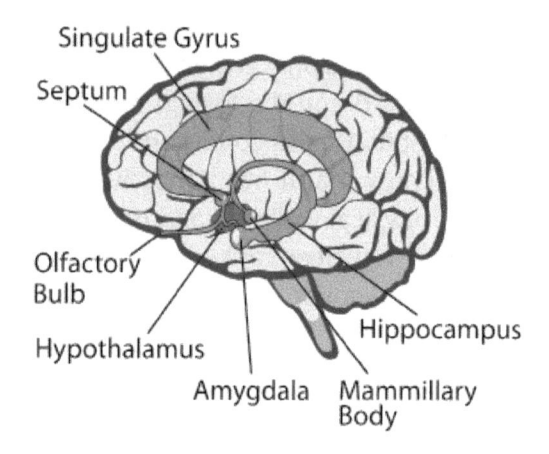

Overview of the brain

- The brain is divided into different parts. The outer layers made up of the cortex.

- We have a right and left hemisphere. The right controls the left side of the body and the left controls the right.

- The corpus callosum joins the 2 hemispheres and enables communication between the two.

- Outside of the brain is grey and is wrinkled

- Inside of the brain is white and smooth due to them having an insulating layer of Myelin.

What the brain is made up of

- Brain Stem - this is the oldest part of the brain, it's the animal part of us. It monitors threat and reacts to threat

- Cerebellum - this is our little brain. It takes all the data from our sensory systems and translates the environment we are in. It governs movement.

- Occipital Lobe - this is our visual field, it helps processes everything we see.
- Parietal Lobe - this is our sensory motor cortex. It receives and processes info about temperature, taste, touch and movement coming from the rest of the body.
- Frontal Lobe - this is what makes us human! Our reasoning, logic, intelligence, creativity, mood, planning for the future, setting goals and judging priorities.
- Temporal Lobe where we find the Limbic system - houses our emotions, processes hearing, memory and language functions our Limbic system.
- The image on the right shows the location of the Limbic system within the brain. It contains a number of structures the ones we are concerned with are the Amygdala and the Hippocampus.
- Amygdala - is involved with emotion, learning and memory. It's part of the system that processes "reflexive" emotions like fear and anxiety. This is our inbuilt alarm system.
- Hippocampus - is involved with the formation of long term memories and is important for our recovery and healing.

Central Nervous System
- The brain uses the central nervous system as the tool to communicate to our bodies to keep us safe and alive and to thrive.
- Sympathetic Nervous system is our Fight /Flight / Freeze/ Flop / Friend response
- Para-sympathetic Nervous system is our rest / digest / re-generate and learn response
- Cannot be in both at the same time

Reptilian Brain

- The brain stem - our animal instinct - sits inside the Temporal lobe.
- When the temporal lobe (hearing/memory/ language) fires up - the frontal lobe (reasoning/logic/intelligence/creativity) switches off
- Emotions take over and we are then in a reactionary state
- We are never in both at once - SNS Response

Why do we need to know this?

- The animal brain; the reptilian brain only cares about fight/flight/freeze/food/fornicate and Safety
- It does not think, it is immediate and reaction dominate.
- When the reptilian brain is activated so is the Hippocampus (responsible for memories, emotions and feelings) in the Limbic system
- What gets fired together gets wired together (however long term stress will cause the Hippocampus to go offline causing post traumatic stress responses or PTSD.
- We can only feel human again when the 'animal' is safe.
- Threat in any form is carbohydrate intensive. The body demands oxygen and sugar NOW!
- If your brain and body are in a constant state of stress / high alert and there is no real threat anymore......there will be consequences to you depending on the way you deal with your threats.
- You need therapy and/or a place of safety when you are in this state of being

Temporal Lobe/Paleomammalian Brain

- This is our emotional brain
- Every experience we have we learn from

- You can take yourself out of 'fear' by learning how to turn off your alarm system and bringing your Hippocampus back online by understanding where you are, assessing your safety, are you really under threat? Moving yourself into your human brain/Frontal Lobe through mindfulness.

Frontal Lobe/Neomammalian Brain

- This is newest / youngest or immature brain
- It is slow, plodding and thoughtful
- It accepts rules, boundaries and laws
- You only live in this 'brain' when you are under no threat to your survival
- This is where you thrive; you cannot thrive if your alarm system is constantly on and your Hippocampus is offline.

How the brain develops

- Newborn - during foetal development 100billion neurons are created
- These migrate to different areas of the brain
- They specialise in response to chemical signals
- The primitive brain develops first (brain stem/mid brain) followed by the Limbic (paleomammalian) and cerebral cortex (neomammalian)
- At birth the Reptilian brain is fully functioning, the newborn can breathe, eat, sleep, see, smell, make noise, feel sensations and recognise people close to them.
- If a mum to be is frightened/stressed whilst pregnant the child brain will already be set up to be more alert, more anxious, more reactive so we need to educate people about the impact of trauma.
- Majority of brain growth and development such as regulating emotions, language and abstract thought takes place after birth.

- Brain development is the process of creating, strengthening and discarding connections among the neurons.
- These connections are called Synapses.
- Synapses organise the brain by creating pathways that connects the parts of the brain governing everything that we do.
- Breathing-sleeping to thinking and feeling
- Synapses develop at fast rate - 2M per sec in a healthy toddler.
- Some of these Synapses are strengthened and remain intact but many are discarded.
- A child of 3 will have 1,000 trillion synapses. By adolescents ½ of the synapses will have been discarded. Only about 50% of Synapses will remain from Adolescents to death.
- However brain development continues throughout the lifespan.
- Mature brain cells are insulated with a white fatty sheath called Myelin. This ensures clear transmission across synapses.
- Neuronal growth processes and myelination will be impacted by a child's experiences.
- Age 3 the brain is 90% adult size
- Brain growth depends on receiving stimulation, stimulation provides the foundation for learning.
- The brain will adapt to its environment be it positive or negative!
- If certain synapses and neuronal pathways are not stimulated and strengthened, they may be discarded and the capabilities that they promised maybe discarded.
- E.g. Infants have a strong predisposition to create a strong bond with their primary caregivers. If this does not happen the child's ability to form any health relationship during their lifetime maybe impaired.

- Building an efficient network of pathways is crucial for normal growth and development
- When repeated experiences strengthen a neuronal pathway, the pathway becomes encoded and it eventually becomes a memory.
- The creation of memories is us adapting to our environment, our interactions with the world that promotes our survival and growth.
- If early environment is abusive or neglectful we will create memories that will impact us for the rest of our lives.
- Babies are born with implicit memory - unconscious recall
- At Age 2 they develop explicit memory - conscious recall
- If a child has been abused they may not be able to recall explicit memories but have implicit memories in the form of flashbacks - nightmares or other uncontrollable reactions
- Our brain continues to grow into and develop into young adulthood.
- Before puberty there is a growth spurt in the frontal lobe (planning/impulse control and reasoning)
- During teenage years and young adulthood the brain prunes synapses and develops more myelin to insulate the nerve fibres and speed up neural processing.
- If a child is abused the brain can be altered by this
- Toxic stress, resulting in negative impacts on the child's physical, cognitive, emotional and social growth.
- The neuronal pathways that are developed and strengthened under negative conditions prepare children to cope in that negative environment and their ability to respond to nurturing and kindness maybe impaired.

Long-term effects of abuse and neglect on the developing brain

- Smaller left hemisphere - increase risk of depression
- Irritability in the Limbic system (F/F/F) - increase in panic / anxiety / PTSD
- Smaller growth in the Hippocampus and Limbic - increase risk of DID and memory impairments

'DAMAGED CHILDREN OFTEN GROW UP TO BE DAMAGED ADULT'

By this I mean if we do not get the help and support we need to recover and fulfil our true potential the impact of child abuse on us as victims and survivors will impact everyone around us including our children. I am to my knowledge the 3rd generation of abuse happening within the extended family - this is truly a horrifying reality but not an uncommon one.

My dad said he was abused, my mum was abused. They were both in a domestic violence relationship together, we the kids suffered as a result. My dad entered into another abusive relationship with the step mum. My dad abused her kids, she abused us; we suffered as a result. My mum entered into another abusive relationship with the stepdad and they both abused us. As you can see there is lots of poor parenting and dysfunction - how are earth are we the children meant to grow up and become model parents ourselves if we have not experienced nurture, love, care, protection and growth????

At some stage we need to break the cycle of poor parenting and dysfunction. Often victims and survivors of childhood abuse who become parents do not know how to provide everything their children need because they have not experienced it themselves. This is not a criticism of our parenting skills but a real issue that exists and one which can be addressed with the right knowledge and support.

I have found it extremely hard to cuddle or kiss people on the cheek. Saying hello or goodbye will be a handshake and many find this weird. I was able to cuddle my children when they were small and vulnerable but as they have grown up I find it hard to be spontaneous in cuddling them. I cuddle when I want to; not when they want to. I can see that this hurts my daughter sometimes. I am actively working on this!

I know that in many households shouting is commonplace and is a result of frustration and anger. If you have grown up in a household like this you will often resort to this behaviour yourself unless you have recognised that it's one of your triggers and you don't like it or you know the impact of shouting can cause major stress on your children so you don't do it.

What does a normal childhood look like? NSPCC & Chris Theisen - The Parent Coach Plan

NSPCC Definition (www.nspcc.org.uk/):

- Children need adequate food, water, shelter, warmth, protection and health care.
- They also need their carers to be attentive, dependable and kind.
- Children are neglected if these essential needs - the things they need to develop and grow - are persistently not met.

According to Chris Theisen, the creator of The Parent Coach Plan (http://www.parentcoachplan.com/), there are eight essential responsibilities that parents must adhere to in order to foster their child's physical and/or emotional well-being.

Parents have 8 Key Responsibilities:

- Safe environment - physical home, free from abuse and feel safe in caregivers company
- Basic needs - water, food, shelter, warmth, medical care, appropriate clothing, and their own space
- Build up their self esteem - acceptance of your child/praise their achievements and use discipline as a time to teach them right from wrong.

- Teach them morals and values - honesty, respect, responsibility, compassion, patience and generosity

- Develop mutual respect - respect their privacy, feelings and opinions, individuality

- Provide discipline - structured, predictable and fair

- Be involved in your child's education - recognise their achievements, homework and if needs be get them help.

- Get to know your child - communicate with them and spend quality time with them

Please check out *Parenting without Tears*, a guide written by me for victims and survivors who want to be the best parents they can be.

http://www.amazon.co.uk/Parenting-without-Tears-Chris-Tuck-ebook/dp/B00E0NO95U

What happens when abuse/trauma occurs? Understanding the impact of trauma on your brain (mental health) and your body (physical health) and the 'Stress Response'.

a. **What is abuse? What is trauma?**

b. **Your alarm system - what is this?**

- The Amygdala and Hippocampus
- The Stress Response

a. **What is abuse?**

- Abuse is all about Power and Control.
- The perpetrator is often in a position of power and control.
- The victim is stripped of any power and control that they may have had. This is a constant threat to their survival.

- The survivor often spends a lifetime trying to regain power and control over themselves and their life.

- Having no power or control over what is happening to you will lead victims/survivors of abuse to seek out something to help them cope with their situation.

- The unexpressed pain and emotions will either make the individual implode or explode.

What is trauma?

- Trauma can be a threat to our life, a serious injury or an attack on our physical integrity.

- It involves intense fear, helplessness and or horror.

- It can be a single one event or repeated multiple events.

- Child sexual abuse commonly consists of a series of traumatic events over an extended period of time and includes sexual assault, physical violence, emotional abuse and neglect.

- To aid survival the brain releases a cascade of neuro-chemicals which start a complex chain of body reactions. This helps to cushion the trauma and helps you deal with what is happening. This survival response acts outside your conscious control meaning you have no control over it. You are not at fault or to blame on how your body responds to child sexual abuse.

b. Your alarm system - What is this? How does it work?

I decided to show you how your alarm system works in a flowchart (on the following page) format to make it easier to understand and digest!

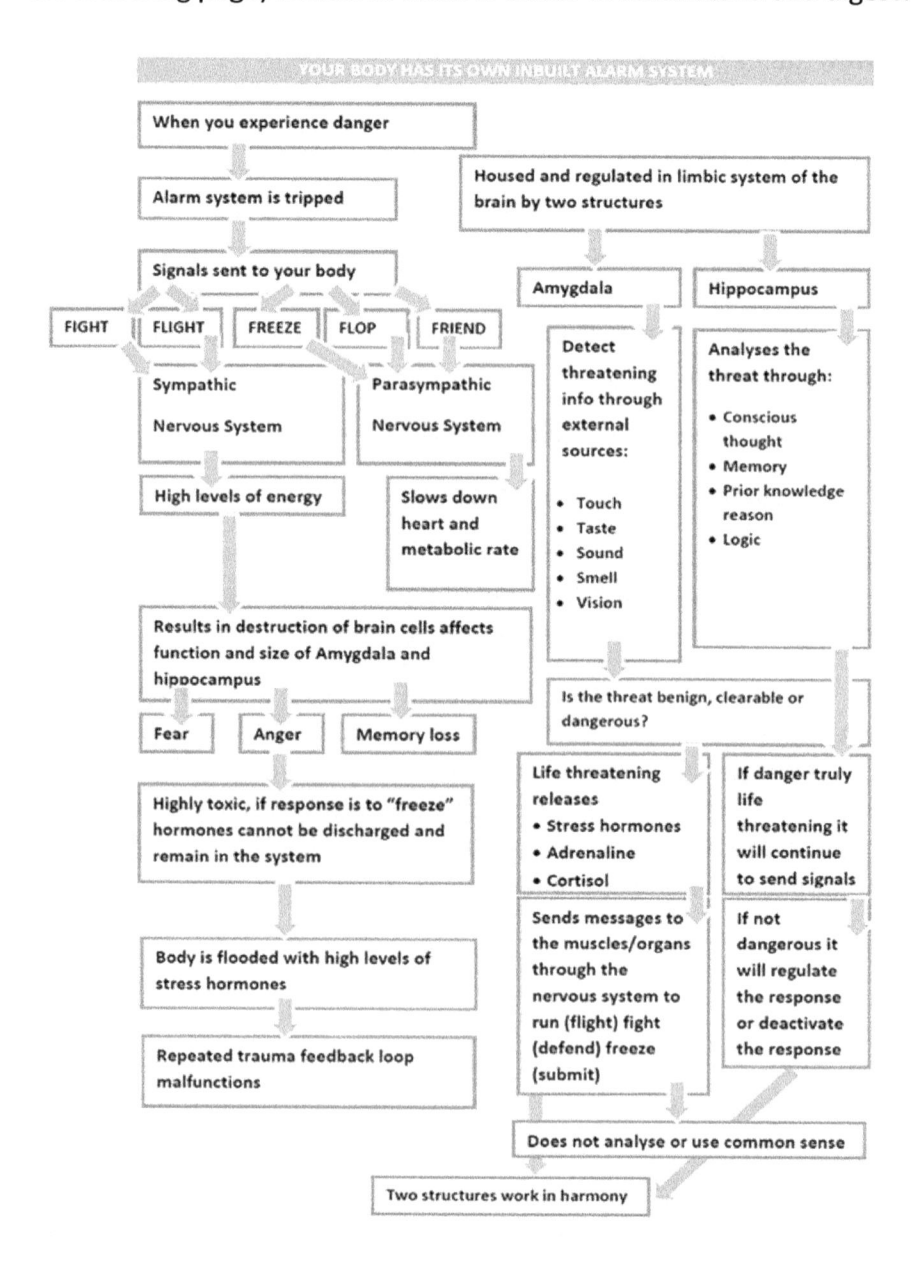

YOUR BODY HAS ITS OWN INBUILT ALARM SYSTEM

When you experience danger

↓

Alarm system is tripped

Housed and regulated in limbic system of the brain by two structures

↓

Signals sent to your body

Amygdala | **Hippocampus**

FIGHT | FLIGHT | FREEZE | FLOP | FRIEND

Amygdala — Detect threatening info through external sources:
- Touch
- Taste
- Sound
- Smell
- Vision

Hippocampus — Analyses the threat through:
- Conscious thought
- Memory
- Prior knowledge reason
- Logic

Sympathic Nervous System → High levels of energy

Parasympathic Nervous System → Slows down heart and metabolic rate

Results in destruction of brain cells affects function and size of Amygdala and hippocampus

Fear | Anger | Memory loss

Is the threat benign, clearable or dangerous?

Highly toxic, if response is to "freeze" hormones cannot be discharged and remain in the system

Life threatening releases
- Stress hormones
- Adrenaline
- Cortisol

If danger truly life threatening it will continue to send signals

Body is flooded with high levels of stress hormones

Sends messages to the muscles/organs through the nervous system to run (flight) fight (defend) freeze (submit)

If not dangerous it will regulate the response or deactivate the response

Repeated trauma feedback loop malfunctions

Does not analyse or use common sense

Two structures work in harmony

As you can see from this flowchart our inbuilt alarm system housed in the Limbic system is there for our protection. The Amygdala is the primitive animal brain and detects threat. The Hippocampus analyses the threat and has control over the Amygdala. You can clearly see that the brain has direct control over the body on a sub conscious level.

The Amygdala and Hippocampus work in harmony with each other. When a threat is detected by the Amygdala, neuro-chemicals are released to prepare your body for the fight / flight / freeze / flop / friend response. The Hippocampus will continue to send signals to the Amygdala whilst the threat continues or it will deactivate the response once it passes. The mind and body will then revert back to normal.

Your stress response

This is the normal threat - reaction cycle = Stress Response.

However with repeated trauma this feedback loop malfunctions and the body becomes flooded with high levels of stress hormones. Here is another flowchart showing what happens:-

WHEN ALARM DEFAULT SETTING IS ON

Body is flooded with chronic levels of stress hormones

⬇

HIPPOCAMPUS GOES OFFLINE
- Cannot evaluate levels of danger
- Or whether danger is internal or external
- Or whether traumatic event is over or ongoing

⬇

Cannot send deactivation signal to the Amygdala to turn off alarm system

⬇

Alarm system constantly on and the stress hormones continue to flood the body

⬇

Body thinks the traumatic event is ongoing even after is has ceased

⬇

You will act as thought you are being repeatedly traumatised

⬇

Leads to a heightened sense of danger

⬇

HYPER-AROUSAL

⬇

Results PTS Responses

The Amygdala and the Hippocampus

From the above flowchart you can see what happens when the body is flooded with stress hormones continuously. The Hippocampus goes offline and cannot control the Amygdala. Your body thinks the traumatic event is still happening even though it has ceased. Over time this can lead to Hyper-arousal and Post Traumatic Stress responses or PTSD.

The Hippocampus has an important role to play in storing memories and processing new experiences and storing these as memories.

If the Hippocampus is offline it cannot process experiences. Unprocessed experiences whether they be real or a 'trigger' are alive, demanding attention. They will remain as frightening as when you first experienced them unless you deal with them and to do that your brain needs to feel safe; not under threat.

In the next flowchart, you can see visually how the Hippocampus is affected.

```
┌─────────────────────────────────────┐
│            HIPPOCAMPUS              │
│                                     │
│  Cannot turn off alarm system. It cannot store │
│    new memories. Trauma cannot be stored       │
│    within context online making it seem        │
│       continuous and never ending.             │
└─────────────────────────────────────┘
                    ↓
┌───────────────────────────────────────────────────────┐
│ Keeps the trauma online with the same distress and intensity as when actual │
│                      assault happened                  │
└───────────────────────────────────────────────────────┘
                    ↓
┌───────────────────────────────────────────────────────┐
│     The Hippocampus stores new memories and experiences │
└───────────────────────────────────────────────────────┘
                    ↓
┌───────────────────────────────────────────────────────┐
│            Memory is a necessary ait to survival        │
└───────────────────────────────────────────────────────┘
                    ↓
┌───────────────────────────────────────────────────────┐
│     Memory stores both positive and negative experiences │
│         Positive/Pleasurable – Negative/unpleasant       │
└───────────────────────────────────────────────────────┘
```

```
        ↓                                    ↓
┌──────────────────────┐          ┌──────────────────────┐
│ Stored so they can be │          │ Stored so they can be │
│       repeated        │          │       avoided         │
└──────────────────────┘          └──────────────────────┘
                    ↓
┌───────────────────────────────────────────────────────┐
│ Memory constantly adds and subtracts when integrating new experiences in to │
│                      past experiences                  │
└───────────────────────────────────────────────────────┘
                    ↓
┌───────────────────────────────────────────────────────┐
│ We process experiences by reviewing them, elaborating them, linking them to │
│                      other experiences                 │
└───────────────────────────────────────────────────────┘
                    ↓
┌───────────────────────────────────────────────────────┐
│     Allows them to be stored as memories to direct future behaviour │
└───────────────────────────────────────────────────────┘
                    ↓
┌───────────────────────────────────────────────────────┐
│ As you process experiences you will be able to make them less frightening by │
│                reducing their emotional intensity       │
└───────────────────────────────────────────────────────┘
                    ↓
┌───────────────────────────────────────────────────────┐
│ Saving your document to a folder to access later rather than leaving it online │
│     waiting for your attention every time you access your computer │
└───────────────────────────────────────────────────────┘
                    ↓
┌───────────────────────────────────────────────────────┐
│ Unprocessed experiences are hard to store in memory because they we always │
│   demand attention, will remain as frightening as when you experience them │
└───────────────────────────────────────────────────────┘
```

Your Hippocampus needs to come back online in order to be able to tell the Amygdala that the threat is no longer there and to turn off the stress hormones.

Triggers

To enable this to happen we need to look at our 'Triggers' and deal with our intrusive memories, nightmares and flashbacks.

When you suffered a traumatic event you may have seen, felt, touched, smelt, tasted or heard certain things and now after the event you may be triggered by something you see, you feel, you touch, you smell, you taste or you hear that is the same or similar to the original traumatic event. If the trigger is too upsetting you may avoid recalling it either by suppression or distraction. If you do not process the memory it remains vivid or frightening and comes back to you via intrusive memories, flashbacks and or nightmares.

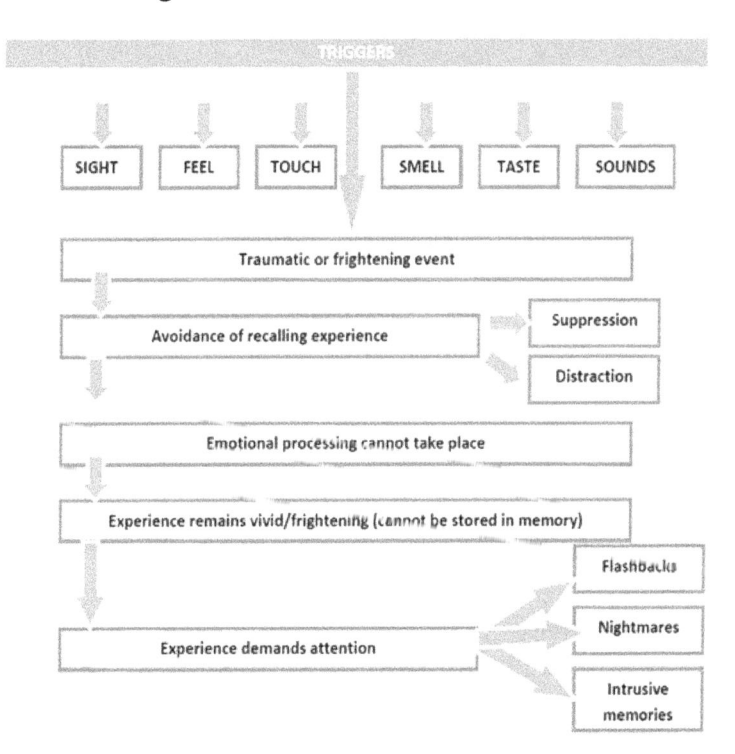

TRIGGERS

SIGHT | FEEL | TOUCH | SMELL | TASTE | SOUNDS

Traumatic or frightening event

Avoidance of recalling experience → Suppression

Distraction

Emotional processing cannot take place

Experience remains vivid/frightening (cannot be stored in memory)

Experience demands attention → Flashbacks

Nightmares

Intrusive memories

As you can clearly see if we do not deal with our triggers, our intrusive memories, flashbacks, nightmares our brain will always sense and detect threat and our bodies will respond accordingly with the 'Stress Response'. This has a massive impact on our both our mental and physical health.

How to deal with intrusive memories

There are two ways that we can deal with intrusive memories either by processing them with specialist support or by blocking them through dissociation and self sabotage.

The only way we can recover our full health, wellness and happiness is my learning to process our intrusive memories; so that we can bring our Hippocampus back on line, turn off our alarm system, stop releasing stress hormones and to restore inner calm and peace!

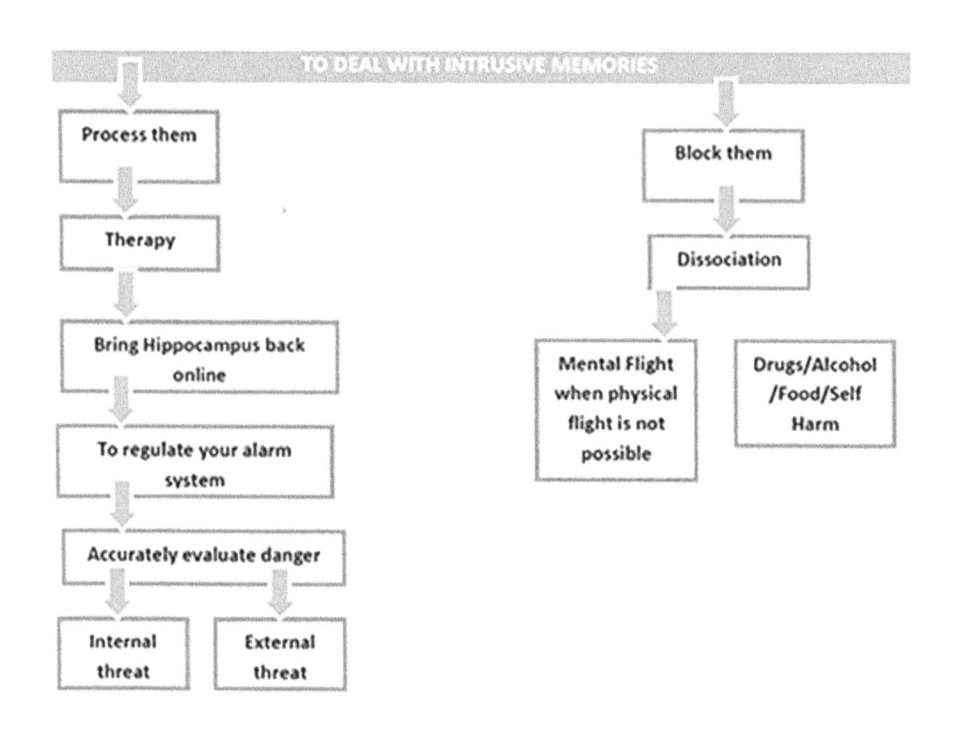

TO DEAL WITH INTRUSIVE MEMORIES

Process them → Therapy → Bring Hippocampus back online → To regulate your alarm system → Accurately evaluate danger → Internal threat / External threat

Block them → Dissociation → Mental Flight when physical flight is not possible / Drugs/Alcohol/Food/Self Harm

High levels of circulating stress hormones

The flowchart below shows you the impact of high levels of circulating stress hormones can have on your mental and physical health.

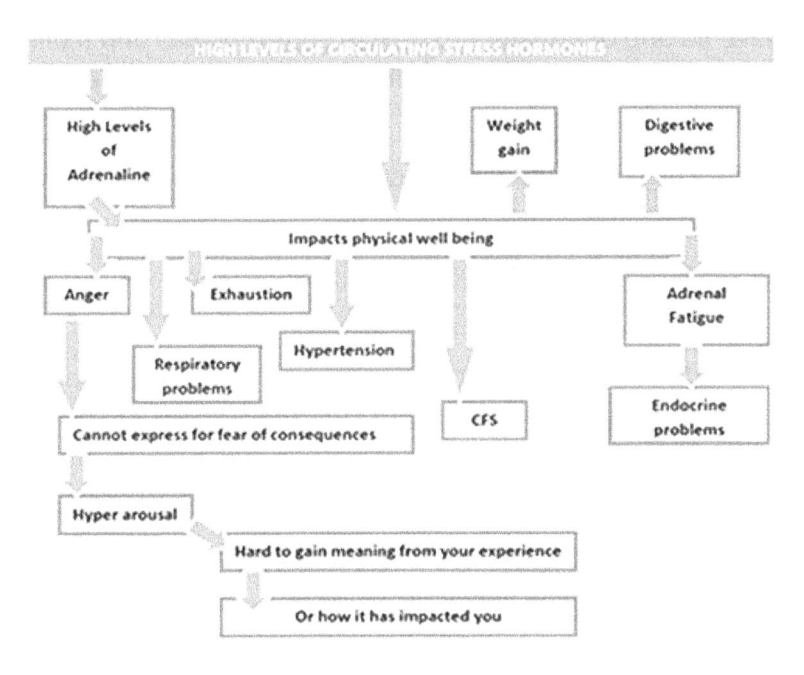

HIGH LEVELS OF CIRCULATING STRESS HORMONES

- High Levels of Adrenaline
- Weight gain
- Digestive problems

Impacts physical well being

- Anger
- Exhaustion
- Hypertension
- Respiratory problems
- CFS
- Adrenal Fatigue
- Endocrine problems

Cannot express for fear of consequences

Hyper arousal

Hard to gain meaning from your experience

Or how it has impacted you

Remember what I said to you earlier on in *My top tips to make change* about speaking up and speaking out?

Not everyone feels that this is the right thing to do.

However I completely disagree if you are being impacted, affected by the abuse you have suffered the only way to make your brain feel safe and to stop the stress response is to talk about how you are feeling and why with a specialist support service i.e. a professional(s) who understands the impact of trauma.

4. What can we do to help ourselves?

When you have negative thoughts and feelings going around in your head constantly it can make you very unwell, exhausted and unhappy.

If you have no one or nowhere to offload your thoughts and feelings to this can trigger your alarm system and set off the 'stress response' and hormonal cascade.

To start to change your thoughts and feelings you need to find ways of bringing some lightness back into your life.

I now have a few activities for you to complete to see if we can achieve this.

WARNING If you find that you cannot do these activities at this moment in time - that's fine please just continue to read and come back to them if and when you want to.

If you are finding that you are becoming overwhelmed or triggered please go and speak to your GP or contact a service in the back of this book for further guidance, help and support.

A fantastic book that may help you that I have referred to throughout this PILLAR of health is *The Warrior Within* book by Christiane Sanderson written for the One in Four charity (http://www.oneinfour.org.uk/the-warrior-within/).

Activity 1 - 25 Smiles

Do you find that as we grow older - due to worries, stress, mortgages, rental payments, work, and family life - we get bogged down and forget about us, our laughter and what makes us smile?

This exercise is all about remembering old ways or finding new ways to bring some of the light heartedness back into our lives. We often feel weighed down by our troubles, especially if our life is filled with anxious thoughts or the guilt and shame of abuse.

Permit yourself time to smile, start by asking yourself what makes you feel happy.

Ask yourself this question:

What things do you most like to see, hear, taste or smell that make you smile? Think about those things that make you smile regularly and write them down here: I have done my top 5; now you do yours!

1. My kids
2. My dog
3. Doing a fitness class
4. Feeling the sun on my skin
5. Hearing the sea

Activity 2 - Your funeral

TRIGGER If you are feeling suicidal please skip this activity. Check the back of the book for Helplines that you can call if you need to.

I know, it sounds a bit grim doesn't it? And you're probably thinking what has this activity got to do with child abuse or recovery?? That's what I thought!

But wait, this activity is amazing and will really get you thinking ... a lot. It also makes you think deeply about yourself, your values and your actions.

How does it work? I hear you ask!

Well you need to imagine you are at your own funeral - at your wake in fact.

You are surrounded by family, friends and colleagues.

You are listening to what they are saying about you.

Now I want you to write down what you would like them to say about you.

- You may not care what some relatives or certain people think about you and that is OK.

- But you may have some relationships that you want to improve on and this activity will highlight the importance of these people in your life.

- Does their opinion of you really matter to you?

- If not, then you need to find a way to heal from that. Usually this will be just acceptance of the situation. 'Healing through leaving'.

- If yes, than you will need to find a way of dealing with the issues to be able to reconnect and rebuild a relationship on a smaller level or you may need to try family counselling or a mediator.

Let's start with your closest family … and when you are ready with that pen in your hand, complete the ones that are relevant to you: (exclude the abuser).

Your son

Your daughter

Your husband

Your wife

Your mum

Your dad

Your sister

Your brother

Your aunts

Your uncles

Your in-laws

Let's move onto your close friends. Who are they?

What would you like them to say about you?

Let's move onto your work colleagues. Who are they?

What would you like them to say about you?

Now that you have a comprehensive list of what you would like said about you.

Re-do the exercise detailing what you think they are actually saying about you.

Did you complete this activity in full?

If not, go back and take time out to complete it.

Did you notice any differences?

Are you the person now that you want to be remembered for?

Yes?

Then congratulations you are doing a fantastic job.

No?

What do you think you need to do to change their opinion of you?

What action can you take now to change what is being said at your funeral?

It's all in your hands.

You have the power to turn your life around and live the life of your dreams by being the person you want to be remembered for.

When I first came across the activity I thought my mentor was having a laugh! I completed this activity under duress but it's the only one that has stayed with me for years. From this activity I learned who was important to me and why.

I learnt that I wanted my life to count for something. I was not going to die a nobody. I was going to make something of myself despite my upbringing and adversity.

This activity put a fire in my belly to truly focus and achieve, to give back where I can but more importantly to make each day count.

It highlighted my purpose and showed me that my passion would help me succeed with my purpose.

My reason for being here.

The reason why I experienced what I did.

I would love to know what this activity does for you! Drop me line @ sobbtc@outlook.com

Activity 3 - The Promise/Achievement Jar

This is an opportunity to think about the promises you make to yourself and the way you reward or treat yourself. Have a think about this for a minute

Do you make yourself promises?

Do you reward yourself? When was the last time you gave yourself a treat? How does the thought of treating yourself make you feel?

Keeping promises to yourself and recognising your achievements helps build your self-worth and your self-esteem.

We tend to hold a lot of negativity about ourselves, sometimes born from what we were told when we were younger, whether by siblings, parents or bullying at school.

Whilst focusing on the negative we reduce our positive thoughts and experiences, creating a negative balance in our lives - literally making us feel rubbish about ourselves.

Making ourselves think we don't deserve or we are not worthy of treats and nice things in our lives.

We aren't striving for a perfection of balance, but to tip the scales the other way, to be more aware of ourselves, our happiness, be kinder to ourselves and to others.

How can we achieve this?

Where can we begin?

A simple activity today, to carry through to the remainder of the programme is for you to create your own Promise / Achievement Jar.

Create your own Promise / Achievement Jar - using an empty, clean jar or container. Decorate it to make it personal to you.

Write on a strip of paper each time you complete a promise or a small activity. It's just for you, no one is judging you. These are the little things that are important to you.

Simple tasks like:

- Brushing your teeth twice a day
- Going for a daily walk
- Making a meal a day from scratch
- Washing the car
- Meditating
- Stretching
- Having a relaxing bath
- Drinking more water
- Drinking one less coffee a day
- Eating one less biscuit a day

To more complex goals like:

- Achievement of your 7 PILLARS
- Time management
- Gaining a qualification
- Gaining employment
- Ending a relationship
- Starting a new relationship
- Improving communications within one or more of your relationships

Your tasks and goals can be anything that is specific to you.

It's all about recording all achievements of the promises you have made to yourself.

Each task or goal completed will rebuild your self-esteem and start addressing the balance of positivity in your life.

As with all of this it takes consistent and persistent practice. So stick with it!

Activity 4 - Goal Setting

Part of your healing journey will involve 'goal setting' at some stage.

The fact that you are embarking on a journey suggests that there is an ultimate goal - your destination's end but there will be smaller goals - stops along the way.

Once we are able to control our 'alarm system' and our 'stress response' we will be able to move forward with our lives. There will be room for growth and development.

When your brain and your body is not in 'fight, flight' mode; when you are calm and beginning to love life you will be open to positive thoughts and feelings about the future.

Let's look at how we can put our thoughts into an action plan that will help us move forwards.

A thought becomes an action

When you think

- that thought becomes a feeling
- the feeling becomes an emotion
- the emotion creates an action
- when you take enough action you achieve what you want.

Let's look at a practical example

a. Decide on a specific GOAL you want to achieve

GOAL: I want to move from victim to survivor or survivor to thrive

b. You need to have a 'big enough why' to achieve your specific goal

You need to ask yourself 'Why' do you want to move from victim to survivor or survivor to thriver?

You need to dig down and explore your reasons for wanting change

Your answers maybe:

- I am in pain - I want to be free of pain
- I have no energy - I want more energy
- I'm tired of fighting - I want to have fun
- I'm not enjoying life - I want to enjoy life
- I hate my life - I want to love my life

- I'm existing not living - I want more from my life
- No-one loves me - I want to find someone to love me
- I am a nobody - I want to be a somebody

My next question to this is WHY do you want the above? These answers are not specific enough

Let's take a look at one of the answers above and explore it a bit more

Ultimate Goal:- Moving from victim to survivor to thriver

Why? I want more from my life, I am not a victim, I am a survivor and I want to thrive

'I want to be somebody' - (this is one of my reasons)

Why? I was always told I was a nobody I was thick, stupid and unlovable.

Why was this said to you? Because they were mean, horrible and abusive to me

Why do you need to change if what they said was not true? I know what they said was not true because I know that loving, caring, nurturing parents are not mean and abusive to their kids like they were but I need to prove to myself that I can achieve whatever I set my mind to. I have survived what they did to me and I'm going to thrive in spite of what they tried to do to me.

Let's take a look at another one of the responses above and explore it abut more

You need to start asking yourself the **What, How, Why** questions so that you can peel your onion and get to the root of your 'Big Why'.

Ultimate Goal:- Moving from victim to survivor to thriver

Why? I want more from my life, I am not a victim, I am a survivor and I want to thrive

'I want to be free of pain' - (this is another one of my reasons)

Why? Because it hurts

What hurts? My head, my back, my hips, me - I hurt.

How does the 'pain' affect you?

My responses in no particular order…..

- I eat rubbish
- My mobility is restricted
- I feel miserable and I just want to cry
- Everyone around me is getting fed up with me, my moods and my pain
- They don't understand me and what I have been through
- I have put on weight and none of my clothes fit
- I don't want to feel like this anymore
- I have no energy
- I'm tired all the time

Once you know your deep rooted 'why' - your deep reason for wanting change this will be the catalyst for you to take a step towards your ultimate goal and keep you on your journey when things get tough.

This activity may not be easy for you but the more you do it the more you can help yourself in your healing.

c. You need to consider the 'Price' you need to pay to achieve your goal.

So after you have decided on your ultimate goal (your thought) and peeled your onion to reveal you 'big rooted why' (your feelings) it's time to take action.

You probably thinking yes but how do I that?

You need to consider the price and by this I mean what it is going to take for you to achieve your ultimate goal? What is the 'cost' going to be to you?

- You may need specialist support therapy like Trauma therapy or EMDR
- You may need to read self-help books
- You may need to change your destructive behaviours i.e. your addiction
- You may need to clean up your nutrition
- You may need to learn a new bedtime routine to improve your sleep
- You may need to learn to de-stress your body undoubtedly!

In my experience to live a happier and healthier life and to reach your full potential you will need to

- Learn how to deal with your triggers - intrusive memories, flashbacks, panic attacks, nightmares so you can keep your brain 'safe' and not trigger the 'stress response'
- Learn grounding techniques to keep yourself safe from triggers.
- Seek specialist support therapy to process your triggers
- Join a Peer2Peer Support group for social interaction
- Learn how to de-stress your mind and body

d. Are you willing to pay the price? - taking action!

You need to pay the 'price' day in day out until you reach your ultimate goal. By this I mean you need to **take persistent and consistent action** on your journey to reach your ultimate destination.

The way I looked at this was....

Being a victim took a lot of my energy. The anger, the hurt, the confusion that I felt exhausted me and made me ill.

I now choose to put all of the energy that was consumed in keeping me down and feeling awful into my recovery, into my future.

It's all about me!

And yes I am willing to 'pay the price' because I am worth it and so are you!

So after you have decided on your ultimate goal **(your thought)** and peeled your onion to reveal your 'big rooted why' **(your feelings)** it's time to take action **(consider the price and pay the price)**.

It is that simple!

e. What happens when I reach my 'final' destination?

To be honest and in my experience survivors of abuse never reach a final destination and this is not a bad thing - let me explain.

When your ultimate goal is like 'I want to be an accountant or a nurse' there is an end destination - it's when you receive your qualification.

But we are on a journey of healing and self-discovery we do not know what we are capable of and when we achieve one thing it feels good, it's empowering so we go onto achieve more.

Our journey can be a long one, it can be straight forward or like taking 5 steps forward and 10 steps back. We are all different and we need to acknowledge, accept and embrace this.

Our journey to health and wellness, our journey to reach our full potential……can, will and should last a lifetime.

No one on this planet knows everything!

There will be people reading this book who disagree with some of the things I am saying. And that's OK - it is not going to change me or what I'm trying to achieve.

All I can do is share what I know is right at this moment in time. I, like you will be constantly evolving and growing and when I learn new knowledge and experiences I will continue to pass them on!

What I do know is that you and I as survivors have been through great adversity, we have come through that and we are capable of coming through anything we put our minds to!

The world is yours for the taking, just be brave, step out of your comfort zone and reach for the moon and the stars because you deserve it.

PILLAR 2 - The C.L.E.A.N.E.R™ Living Therapy Programme - LIFESTYLE CHOICES

Under this PILLAR, we are looking at the lifestyle choices you make on a daily basis and their impact on both our mental and physical health.

Before we look at your current lifestyle choices and whether or not they are good for your health and well-being we need to look at how you would like to live your life if you were not encumbered with the impact of the abuse you have suffered.

This PILLAR is all about understanding your feelings, your emotions and your reactions.

We will be looking at:

- Your Average Perfect Day activity
- Understanding your emotions, choices and responsibilities
- How you choose to react to them and taking responsibility for them.

We want to get to the bottom of what's holding you back. We want to look at the choices you make on a daily basis and see if these are moving you towards your goal(s) or taking you further away from your goal(s).

This isn't about what's stopping you from going on your dream holiday or finding your dream job. This is about exploring what you can do for yourself on a regular basis, with or without external help, in order to start living every day as you want it to be.

Are you ready?

The question I am asking you in this activity is:-

How you would like to spend your average perfect day?

Your average perfect day is unique to you. It needs to include the stuff you do on a regular basis, like work, looking after your family, doing the chores, your hobbies etc.

The point of all this is to identify where you can make little changes to your habitual behaviours, the stuff that holds you back, in order to begin to move forwards. We want to get you somewhere close to the life you believe you deserve. The life that you DO deserve.

We're going to begin to identify any treatment that you may need .

We'll start to pick at what scares you. What are your fears and what is holding you back from achieving your average perfect day?

We want to pinpoint the actions you need to take to remove your fears. We can't fix everything at once but with a few changes you can begin to move towards your average perfect day.

Your average perfect day

What is your idea of the average perfect day? Let's start here.

Unless you know what sort of life you are aiming for - in other words unless you have a goal - it's impossible to begin to change. In order to know what needs to change, you need to identify what it is that you want.

I'm not talking about the one perfect day when you can do everything special and celebratory. This is just your average day but how to make it perfect for you.

If I were to wave a magic wand, what would your average perfect day look like?

We all have different dreams and desires that we aspire to. What are yours?

Do you know?

Use this activity to identify what they are and how you can work towards them.

How can you take control of your own life, choices and responsibilities to work towards your perfect day?

Let's start by describing your perfect morning.

You need to really go into detail. This isn't just a basic description.

Here are some ideas to think about:

- What time would you wake up?
- What is the weather like?
- What is your bed like?
- What are you wearing?
- Who is with you or are you on your own?
- Are you going to read, take a shower or perhaps have breakfast in bed?
- What is for breakfast?
- What does your hair look and feel like?
- What about your skin? How does that look and feel?
- What do your joints feel like?
- How is your lower back feeling?
- What are your energy levels like?

I don't want to put too many ideas into your head, since this is all about what your ideas about your perfect morning are. Not mine. So allow yourself to breathe deeply and slowly.

Visualise your perfect morning. Now write it down here:

Now describe your perfect afternoon:

Now describe your perfect evening:

Can you see how going into this much information can affect your decisions and the day ahead of you?

Most of us wake up and think negatively. Or we just accept it's another day and 'get on with it'.

How far away from your average perfect day are you? Don't worry if it seems like it's out of reach. It isn't really that far from where you are now.

What choices do you think you need to make, to move you from your reality - the present moment - to your perfect day as you have described it here?

What actions do you think you need to take to make your choices successful?

Only persistent and consistent action can make your perfect day happen.

You can make it happen.

Do you believe you can make it happen?

You will need to revisit this activity dependent upon where you are on your journey of healing.

Your Emotions, Choices and Responsibilities

What I have to say may sound quiet harsh especially if you are not ready to hear the message yet. Please read the whole chapter, have a think and come back to what I have said.

This PILLAR is all about finding out what is stopping you from moving forwards in your life.

- We will explore the emotions you may be experiencing that are holding you back.
- It's time to take responsibility for how you are feeling and acting.

- It's time to make choices which can take you from negative thinking and behaviour to positive thinking and behaviour.

One issue you may need to consider is who you blame for how you feel. Do you blame someone else for the way your life has turned out?

If you continue to blame others for your current situation i.e. those who have abused you in the past you will not be able to move forward to a happier and healthier life.

You are playing on being the victim.

Of course you cannot be held responsible for the actions of an abuser but you can control your behaviour and emotional response TODAY..

Now.

This is the only way you can move forwards. You cannot change what has happened. No one can change the decisions of the past or the way an abuser has acted. But we can all decide to change the way we respond to it, the way we react do it. It doesn't have to define our lives going forwards.

Taking positive action to get you to where you want to be in life is empowering and shows the abuser(s) you are the one in control. For some it can feel like you have finally won the battle. You choose not to be defined by the abuse. You choose to live free of decisions or choices you regret.

Only you decide what is going to happen next.

People who have suffered trauma from abuse can feel and hold on to the following emotions:

- Guilt
- Self Blame
- Shame
- Anger

They feel dirty, unloved and unwanted.

They feel they deserve to feel all of these emotions or that they deserved the abuse.

We cannot forgive and often internalise our emotions because we don't know how to express them.

Often the abuse is a big secret so expressing how we feel about it is not an option.

There is no-one to turn to, in order to express how we feel.

This internalisation of feelings and unexpressed emotions over time leads to 'chronic stress'.

The mind and body does not differentiate between the stresses that we under.

Our stress can be due to:-

- Our relationships - partner, family, friends or colleagues
- Our nutrition
- Being dehydrated
- Money worries
- Not having a job or having a demanding job or people at work
- Impact of child abuse

Or a multitude of the above.

If you as an individual are overwhelmed by what has happened to you or what you are currently going through or both - your 'stress bucket' - the amount and types of stress you are under will be overflowing. Your alarm system will be triggered and you will not be coping very well.

We all need to be able to keep a stress reserve, if we can't we will end up having a 'breakdown'.

In order to turn off your alarm system you need to offload something from your 'stress bucket'. This may mean changing jobs, your relationships, improving your water intake, changing what you eat, dealing with your unexpressed feelings and emotions.

In the long term it will be tackling all of these things together.

You need to remember however not to change everything at once because this in itself can be stressful and can overwhelm you into doing nothing!

Please read this book through cover to cover before you decide to take any action. You can then decide what you are most comfortable in tackling first.

For example, it maybe that you choose to tackle your water intake before unloading your 'emotional rucksack' because it is easier for you to do right at this moment in time.

You may then move onto exercising more; covered in PILLAR 6.

You may then move onto eating better and eliminating some of the things we are going to discuss that are further stressors on the body; covered in PILLAR 5.

You may be able to do some or all of these practical things for yourself during your recovery or at different stages of your recovery.

Once you start dealing with your unexpressed emotions and feelings the practical things you can do for yourself may take a slide but the more you can do them - being consistent and persistent with your actions - the more you will be helping yourself with your recovery to optimal health and wellness and a happier life which will allow you to reach your full potential.

- Detoxify your brain of your emotional challenges
- Detoxify your body from non foods, drugs and alcohol

For some of your life, or most of your life or for all of your life people have taken from you and they have left you feeling:-

- Worthless, void of all emotion, broken and or angry, bitter and destructive

Or

- Want to achieve and please at all costs

You should have been nurtured, given love, care, positive attention and clear boundaries of what is acceptable or not (discipline).

Let's look at the emotions you may be experiencing one by one. Let's try and understand what each one is and why you may be feeling that emotion.

Your Emotions by Nicola Mendes

An abused child displays a specific phenotype and as such displays a particular set of characteristics. Along with these traits come certain emotions: guilt, blame, shame. Here we will discuss the negative emotions an abused child will experience, as well as treatment methods we can access to help cope with these emotions as an adult survivor of child abuse.

1. Guilt

There are many different theories to determine the origin of the state of guilt or why we experience guilt. However, the general consensus is that this is an emotion which causes behavioural changes and even influences one's personality through a belief that you have contravened moral standards.

What makes this interesting in the field of psychiatry is that the individual can only feel this extremely powerful emotion If he/she had internalised moral values in early childhood.

If no moral standing was developed there is no way the person can violate the values, and thus no guilt can be felt. Given this definition one may question why some children who experience abuse and trauma feel guilt. The abused child will be raised in a family which does not allow for moral development.

However, some abused children will establish an understanding and internalisation of socially accepted rules and values due to their interactions with the outside world and external support systems (e.g. school teachers and friends).

It is these supported children who understand the immorality of the abusive action and will experience emotions of guilt. Although they understand the "wrong" they do not understand they are not the "wrong-doer". Instead the child internalises the guilt believing he/she has done something to deserve the abuse and must be punished.

This is the commonly associated emotion of self-blame.

2. Self-blame

There are two types of self-blame: behavioural self-blame and characterological self-blame.

Individuals who have suffered child abuse will often show the latter, however many cases have been known to display evidence of both types of self-blame.

Behavioural self-blame refers to blame based on the individual's actions, or lack thereof.

This individual will believe he/she is at fault because they did not act in a way to prevent the abuse. Many older children whom felt it was their responsibility to protect their younger siblings experience behavioural self-blame later in life.

Characterological self-blame refers to a feeling of blame stemming from within oneself. This can be seen when the individual believes the abuse was due to a fault in their character or nature. They feel they deserved to be abused because there is something innately wrong with them.

This type of self-blame is more difficult to treat and often associated with self-harm.

There are various theories to explain the reasoning behind why an abused child experiences self-blame, but the most widely accepted is that of conditioning. Conditioning occurs when a stimulus is taught (conditioned) to behave in a certain way when presented with a certain stimulus. In the case of childhood abuse, the child is told he/she is worthless and then assaulted.

Initially the child may question the statement and not understand why the adult would call him/her worthless, but after several instances of being berated and then beaten he/she will begin to take this as a truth.

The child will be conditioned to believe he/she is worthless and as such deserves abuse for this fault in character.

This conditioning may contribute to a low self-esteem and depression in later life.

3. Shame

Shame is used interchangeably with terms such as guilt or blame, however the definition is different as shame refers to an awareness of one being the victim and not the perpetrator or cause of abuse.

Although this is often an unconscious awareness, it is an awareness. Shame can be divided into two categories: basic shame and toxic shame.

Basic shame can be described as psychological scarring. As the identification of victim status is unconscious, it is manifested in the presence of dread and mistrust.

This is due to an underdeveloped level of trust in others. The abused child grows up believing they are inferior and through conditioning and internalising will enter society with this thought. He/she will experience a deep-rooted anxiety and fear that others will reject and berate him/

her in the same manner as the abuser, despite understanding he/she is the victim. This is the base of toxic shame.

Toxic shame builds on this assumed stigma. The individual believes he/she will be abused for being a victim of abuse, and in some cases it can lead to a state of psychological dysfunction beyond mistrust.

Child abuse and subsequent shame have contributed to mood disorders such as bi-polar disorder.

4. Anger

Anger can be felt regardless of whether or not one believes he/she is the cause of abuse.

Anger is defined as a strong feeling of tension and hostility which is usually pre-empted by extreme anxiety or stress.

An episode of abuse is known to cause a great feeling of displeasure and anxiety within the abused child, thus will lead to a degree of anger. The intensity of the anger will depend on the level of anxiety felt. This anxiety is generally caused by a perceived threat to one's being, possessions or moral values.

It has been seen that children and adults will use violence as a catharsis for anger. This knowledge to employ violence as a release may be due to social learning or, according to evolutionary theory, the humans innate primal instinct.

Regardless of the theoretical explanation, anger can contribute to psychological difficulties in later life and the majority of these individuals will have suffered child abuse. It is argued this abuse is the catalyst for these common "anger-related" disorders: Oppositional Defiant Disorder and Conduct Disorder (followed by Anti-Social Personality Disorder in most cases).

Treatments

There are various means to deal with psychological difficulties and the painful emotions which contribute to them. These include different types of therapeutic treatment, as well as some self-help tips.

1. Pharmacological treatment

Pharmacological therapy refers to medication prescribed by medical practitioners, either a G.P or a psychiatrist.

There are various forms of medication that can be prescribed; it is purely dependent on the type of symptoms you are displaying. Child abuse, and the aforementioned emotions, will often contribute to low mood and anxious states.

To combat these behavioural states practitioners will usually prescribe anti-depressants or anxiolytics (mood stabiliser and relieving anxiety). The most common anti-depressant used is Amitriptyline.

Medication maybe needed in the short term to help stabilise how you are feeling however they will not solve the root cause of your problem 'your suppressed feelings, emotions and pain'.

I am not here to tell you to take medication or not this is between you and your GP/Consultant. I just want you to think about all your options and look at other ways of healing instead of taking medication for the long term.

In my experience many people take medication for one symptom and the side effects from that medication will lead onto taking another medication; all of which will impact your hormones and your health and wellness.

2. Cognitive Behavioural Therapy

One of the most popular forms of psychotherapy is that of cognitive behavioural therapy or CBT.

Six sessions of CBT seems to be the standard therapy offered by the G.P upon referral.

Although CBT has its place it is not the right therapy if you are suffering from trauma. When your alarm system has been triggered and the Hippocampus is offline your brain cannot process anything.

CBT employs a technique whereby the patient focuses on the negative thought or belief (cognition) and works towards changing it in an active manner. The therapist will help the patient identify the unrealistic thought (I am worthless), and through some practical exercises help change it.

One of the most effective forms of CBT to assist abuse victims is that of journal writing.

By maintaining a journal the patient is able to communicate and regulate his/her emotions.

The thoughts experienced in everyday situations, and the associated behaviour, are recorded and examined during sessions. By exploring the diary journals together patient and therapist are able to closely identify difficulties and move towards overcoming them.

I love journal writing it takes all the 'worries' or thoughts that are whirling around in my head away. I express my thoughts and feelings on paper and I feel lighter as a result.

3. Counselling/Specialist Support therapies/Trauma Therapy

Counselling is a form of talking therapy. This is where the patient will discuss life events and associated emotions within a counselling setting. The therapist will often use a person-centred approach which means they will listen, And you will share with them your experiences, feelings and emotions and the therapist will help you understand what is going on for you and help you process what it is you need to process.

I will talk about access to help in more detail under Your Choice later in this chapter.

4. Meditation

An alternative form of therapy is meditation. This is a spiritual technique which involves a "cleansing of the mind and soul". Meditation employs techniques such as deep breathing and mantra repetition to act as a catharsis for feelings of anger and anxiety. By using these calming methods the individual is able to raise self-esteem and self-acceptance relinquishing feelings of self-blame and guilt.

I use 'belly breathing' to help with my anxiety and stress. I share this technique with you under PILLAR 7.

5. Self-help groups - Peer 2 Peer Support

Child abuse is not just an experience you have when you are young, it is a lifelong psychological scar. It affects you, your behaviour and your ability to interact with others throughout adolescence and into adulthood.

To assist individuals who are victims of child abuse and trauma (children and adults) self-help groups have been created.

These groups provide information and advice on how to cope with the emotional and psychological turmoil abused individuals face. A simple search on Google will reveal several results, but here are some examples for you:-

S.O.B - http://survivorsofabuse.org.uk/

ShatterBoysUK - www.shatterboysuk.wordpress.com

Your choices

You have the choice. The power is in your hands.

You have an option to live your life differently, to refuse to be held back by the pain of the abuse you suffered. To move forwards.

Of course it isn't easy but it is a choice.

Please ANSWER the following questions honestly:

The answers may be upsetting but they will show you what you are feeling and how these feelings are holding you back.

Question for you:

Is it time for you to let go?

Do you stay wrapped in your own comfort blanket of what you know, even though it makes you miserable, or do you feel it's time to off load your emotional burden and set yourself free?

What does your comfort blanket look like? Your comfort blanket can be anything that you rely on to get you through your daily life. Sometimes this is the devil you know rather than devil you don't! E.g. are you comforting yourself using drugs? Alcohol? Food? Is this really helping you deal with how you are feeling or is it just masking how you are feeling?

What fears do you have about moving forwards?

What story are you telling yourself, that maybe holding you back?

If you are unhappy and in pain. You need to decide to make a change somewhere. It will be up to you where you make this first small change.

Take the first small step to reclaim yourself:-

- Your health
- Your wellness

- Your happiness
- Your life

How you currently live your life and the choices you are making on a daily basis will dictate where you need to begin on your journey of healing.

Do you have an addiction?

The addiction you may have is your coping mechanism to what has happened to you.

It is not you! - But it can consume you!

To change you must first acknowledge that you have this challenge and get specialist support to help you with this. But please bear in mind that your addiction is a behaviour you have adopted to help you cope with the trauma you are experiencing.

The overwhelm from not being able to express what you are thinking and how you are feeling.

In order to deal with the coping mechanism you have adopted to help you cope; you need to deal with the underlying cause (the root cause) of your problem.

In my experience you will need specialist support to help you deal with both your trauma and your coping mechanisms.

Many of our coping mechanisms are self harming and self sabotaging.

When we think of what has happened to us it can make us feel angry, sad, betrayed, unloved, unworthy. When we are in this frame of mind we just want to switch off from it all.

We seek out something to pick us up and make us feel better.

It may be food (sugar), alcohol, drugs, caffeine or cutting! All of these coping mechanisms may give us a high in the short term but in the long term are harmful for our health and well-being.

Over time we will need larger quantities of our 'fix' in order to make us feel better and this can become our default pattern / behaviour for dealing with all the stress that we may encounter throughout our lifetime.

Large quantities of food (sugar)/ trans fats, alcohol, drugs, caffeine over a long period of time will:-

- Increase the inflammation within our bodies
- Impact our hormones
- Impact our energy levels; we will have highs and lows
- Impact our moods; we will suffer from depression and anxiety

This will impact our joint health and cellular health affecting our mental and physical health, our wellness and happiness!

Access to help
Statutory Services

Your first port of call maybe to your GP or A and E if you need crisis treatment.

If you go to your GP, you will be given a 10 minute appointment and you probably will not tell them straight away. You may visit a few times and talk about your symptoms which may vary from appointment to appointment but not the cause of your symptoms.

If this is you, try writing down exactly how you are feeling, what you are thinking and an outline of what you have been through. If you cannot verbalise what you have written just give them your piece of paper.

Your G.P will usually offer you medication in the first instance and refer you to a statutory service if it's available such as 6 weeks of CBT. There is often a waiting list for this service and if you are suffering from trauma it's not the best service for you at this time.

If you access the community mental health team through either your G.P or A and E they are usually only able to offer crisis management i.e. help and support you if you are suicidal but if you are not quite that low there seems to be no additional help available apart from medication and CBT.

My experience of statutory service has not been good. My GP did not understand the impact of child abuse and to be fair at the time neither did I. I was referred to a counsellor who listened to me cry for the 6 hourly sessions that I was allocated.

6 sessions is not enough time for us to get to know our therapist and until we trust them we will not open up. My therapist never spoke to me about anything personal, there was no bond. How could I trust her with my innermost thoughts and feelings? How could I not know if she was going to judge me or think I wasn't a good mum or good at my job?

This is why many individuals do not disclose the abuse they have suffered for fear of judgment and unwelcome intervention from outside agencies or having the stigma of being labelled with a mental health problem.

6 sessions can do more harm than good - If the therapist unlocks something within you it may make your health worse! Because you do not have enough sessions to explore what is going on for you.

I have heard from many victims and survivors who have shared their story with me and most have said the same. Some have been lucky in the treatment they have received but it all depends where you live and if your G.P understands trauma and child abuse.

If you have presenting symptoms such as an addiction you may get a referral or a prescription to help you with the addiction. Most NHS services are oversubscribed and underfunded and have long waiting lists and they do not offer some of the specialised services that we need.

You usually only get to the top of the waiting list if you are very poorly! I worked for a private health care provider and the NHS often referred patients into us because we had the expertise and the capacity.

If you attend an addiction programme and do not deal with the root cause of your problem there is a high risk that you will relapse. Some placements expect you to go cold turkey others will phase you in and give you alternatives whilst you are detoxing. The shock to your liver from going cold turkey if you drink a lot could kill you.

A therapist once said to me that if someone is self medicating to get themselves through the effects of the abuse then asking them to stop the one thing that is helping them would not be the best solution.

I think it is important to identify and acknowledge that the root cause of your addiction is the abuse you suffered as soon as you can so that you get the right specialist help and support you need to deal with both the trauma and your coping strategy which your addiction.

Many individuals who have not had the right course of treatment from the statutory sector either gets referred to the specialist voluntary sector or seeks them out themselves.

Voluntary sector (non profit) or 3rd Sector Services

In my experience most voluntary sector services or 3rd sector services as they are known have the expertise to help victims and survivors but they too are oversubscribed and underfunded massively and have been for decades.

Usually these organisations are founded by victims and survivors who couldn't find the right help and support they needed so they created the service themselves. This is what I have done with S.O.B.

There are support services for men only, women only, children and adolescent only, offenders only, non offending adult and family support to come to terms with what has happened.

The best thing to do to find support for you and your circumstances is to GOOGLE services in your area or call an umbrella organisation's helpline for advice. We have listed some organisations for you to contact in the back of this book.

Voluntary sector organisations literally have to fight for government funds in order to run their services. The government only likes dealing with big organizations; who have track records as well, they are called preferred providers.

If the government doesn't see a need for a service then funds will not be available; if there is a something appearing in the headlines or something becomes a hot potato like FGM (female genital mutilation) or child sexual exploitation then funding will become available because it makes the government look good. But the funding is never enough and can be withdrawn at any time.

Funding for non recent child abuse for adult survivors has never been a priority and with more and more us coming forward this needs to change!

Voluntary sector organisations who have set themselves up to fulfil a need and have a huge demand for their services tell me that funding is a constant source of worry and contention. Many apply for lottery funding or other pots of money but there is no guarantee that they will be allocated any.

To top it all off statutory services often refer into voluntary sector services but no funding follows.

If you are lucky enough to get a place with the voluntary sector service you can usually access up to two years treatment if needed (some survivors have more than this; others less).

I am currently with a voluntary sector organisation - charity and I pay for my therapy. These organisations usually charge £1 for £1000 you earn so treatment can cost from £1 to £50 per session. The charge they make will usually only cover their overheads, training, and supervision . The therapists often work for free.

One of the most important factors in your recovery is about regaining control.

Abuse is all about someone else having power and control over you making you feel inadequate, powerless and weak.

To break this and to recover you need to feel empowered and in control with what is happening to you.

With this in mind I would suggest that you start really taking stock with what is happening in your life, how you think, how you feel and what would you like to be different?

Whilst reading through this book I would start taking down some notes about anything that you feel you want further information on or things that you would like to see change for you.

Don't worry about HOW you are going to it yet just start to think and write it down on a TO DO List for later.

So one of the first things you can do for yourself is to look in the back of this book for specialist support services in your area and make contact with them when you are ready

Or visit your doctor and have a chat with them.

Your responsibilities

Responsibility is the ability to respond to a situation or event.

If nothing changes; nothing changes

If you are unhappy with something in your life and you carry on doing the same things then how can you expect things to improve?

Let's face it, being a grown up is hard work. I certainly didn't sign up for this! And some people are simply not ready for grown up life because their past trauma has not equipped them to be or it is holding them back.

So they resort to behaviours that are self sabotaging. They seek comfort in 'safe' behaviours like food (comfort eating), alcohol, eating disorders or self harm.

Some people just rebel against taking on any responsibility.

Being responsible for something means doing something to achieve an end result.

To take control of your own life you need to be able to make your own choices and to be responsible for the end result. This can be really scary for some people especially if they have never been allowed to think for themselves or allowed to make decisions for themselves before.

Is this you?

You need to take Responsibility for the **YOU** - you want to become. You need to become responsible for the life you want to live.

YOU need to become responsible for turning your life into your average PERFECT DAY.

Are you ready?

It's TIME......

Time for you to start to heal,

Time for you to learn to love yourself,

Time for you to learn to love others,

Time for you to learn to be loved,

Time for you to start to trust,

Time for you to invest in yourself,

Time for you to make something of yourself,

Time for you to grow and evolve,

Time for you to live your life free of pain and doubt,

Time for you to break free of the past,

Time to forgive maybe? Time to forget? - never!

But it is time for you to live a life that you dream of for you, a life that you deserve and are capable of achieving.

PILLAR 3 - The C.L.E.A.N.E.R™ Living Therapy Programme - ENDOCRINE SYSTEM (HORMONES)

Endocrine System (Hormones)

Have you ever had one of those days? When your child tripping over on the way to school or burning a piece of toast has caused you to have what appears to be an over-reactive melt down?

This isn't you. It isn't the burnt toast. It's just the thing that's pushed you over the edge.

Our hormones are complicated. There is a lot to learn and take in when it comes to fully understanding the role our hormones play in our health and recovery. I'm just going to scratch the surface.

Nutrition and fitness, well-being and mindset, your natural state of balance, can all be affected by your hormones and by your hormonal response to events outside and inside of your body. The opposite is also true, your hormones can be affected by your fitness and mindset and also by your lifestyle choices.

In Pillar 1 we looked at how our mind and body is affected by triggers, we explored the 'stress response' and the impact that this has on our hormones.

There are some very simple things you can incorporate into your lifestyle in order to begin to change your hormonal balance. Victims and survivors of abuse often suffer from chronic stress; stress that has accumulated in the body over many years.

Sleep, exercise, relaxation and diet are very basic ways of altering your hormone balance.

What are hormones?

Hormones act as a chemical messaging system in our bodies. There are different types of hormones in our body that are released and this is dictated by our food, drink, activity levels and generally what we do.

Our hormones regulate our:-

- Body development
- Sexual function
- Reproduction
- Mood
- Appetite
- Metabolism (how we get energy from food)

How do they work?

Hormones travel into our bloodstream, tissues and organs and act as traffic lights. They tell our cells when it is time to slow down or speed up.

You can change all of the above when you de-stress your body and change your nutrition and your physical activity for the better and conversely you can encounter stress and overwhelm and eat poorly, not exercise and this can impact you negatively.

Hormones balance each other out through our blood sugar levels.

When we are stressed we release cortisol (the stress hormone) to balance our cortisol the body releases insulin.

Insulin is also released when we eat sugary foods so when we are stressed it's common for our hormones to send a message to our brain and stomach to say we want some sugar!

Stress = cortisol release = insulin release = demand for sugary foods

The more sugar you have the more sugar you crave.

If you eat more foods (sugary foods) that produce insulin on a regular basis you will experience the following:

- You will crave more of that food and become addicted
- Your taste receptors will become dominant (you will not like other foods)
- In the long term your liver and pancreas will dysfunction - Type 2 diabetes
- Your energy levels will fluctuate - when you become tired and lethargic you will crave more sugary foods = more insulin to get you out of a dip.
- You will store more body fat
- The circulation of your blood becomes more difficult leading to heart related problems.
- Your mood will change regularly.

For the purposes of this book, we are only going to discuss cortisol. It's the biggest culprit when it comes to a life affected by anxiety or stress.

Cortisol

Understanding cortisol can be a real breakthrough when you are in a cycle of self-harm or anxiety.

Once you understand how it works and when it is working (often too hard) in your body, you can begin to take measures to redress the balance.

Cortisol is your stress hormone. You've probably heard it mentioned before. Cortisol is secreted by the adrenal glands which are small glands sitting on top of the kidneys.

Your cortisol levels are affected by lack of sleep, diet, exercise, caffeine, smoking, lack of relaxation, fear, allergies and other stresses like marital or financial worries.

Cortisol is responsible for the fight or flight response. Or as I like to call it, the fight, flight, freeze flop or friend response.

The problem with cortisol is that when we are in a stressed out state for a long period of time, cortisol can be over-active. In this state, the slightest thing can tip us over the edge - as in my burnt toast example. Suddenly we go from a stressed out but coping state, to a feeling of worthlessness with low self-esteem.

Even though I have not discussed all the other hormones with you here (because again I could write a book on them!) I want to just say to you that if you address your stressors which include your mindset, your nutrition, your fluid intake, you activity levels, your sleep, your rest and regeneration your hormones will balance themselves out!

Here is a list of the most important hormones that you might want to look into.

- Oestrogen
- Leptin
- Insulin
- Ghrelin
- Growth hormone
- Oxytocin
- Testosterone
- Progesterone

Below is the hormonal cascade, it shows how some of the hormones inter-relate and how this will not only affect your mental and physical health, but your size and shape.

The Hormonal Cascade

Normally our stress hormone Cortisol should be low overnight whilst Testosterone (T) and our Growth Hormone (GH) should be high allowing for repair and replenishment.

If our Cortisol levels are high due to being overstressed, overworked, overtired then T and GH will be low. If T and GH are low then our Estrogen (E) levels will be high.

Estrogen (E) affects the Thyroid, if (E) is high then thyroid is low.

Thyroid affects the metabolism; if our metabolism is not working correctly then our ability to drop weight/fat is compromised.

Poor sleep is down to high cortisol levels, popping a pill will not address the root cause.

We need to balance out our stress hormones. We can do this through our diet, eating cruciferous vegetables such as broccoli, cauliflower, kale and pak choi which helps detoxify the body and balance the stress hormones.

Adrenal Fatigue

Tipping the balance too far in the 'stressed out' direction when your alarm system is continuously switched on can result in adrenal fatigue. This is a very big topic and is also very common in people who are suffering from chronic stress.

To give you some idea of what adrenal fatigue is (and whether you've experienced it) you may have times when you feel wired but tired. (Too much energy but you are exhausted)

Perhaps you have trouble falling asleep even though you are exhausted and then you struggle to get up in the morning.

You might find yourself feeling tired again by 9am and your sluggishness means it takes longer to get things done.

By around 6pm, when you should be winding down you're ready to go again. On full energy.

If you have adrenal fatigue you probably don't handle stress well and your sex drive is reduced. You might also crave salty foods and take more time to recover from illness.

If you have suffered abuse you maybe have the added burden of experiencing:-

- Triggers
- Intrusive memories
- Nightmares
- Flashback
- Panic attacks
- Hyper arousal
- Dissociation

Which will only make the adrenal fatigue worse.

Does this sound like you now or something you've experienced in the past?

The great news about adrenal fatigue is that changes in your diet and routine, including relaxation and having an awareness of how you feel can make a big difference to your recovery. However if you are impacted with Post Traumatic Stress (PTS) responses you will need to deal with these alongside or before the other changes you wish to make to your current lifestyle.

Becoming more aware of the fact that you can change situations and take time out for yourself can also begin to affect your adrenal response and your recovery.

Understanding your triggers

Whether you are a victim of abuse or you are suffering from an anxiety disorder you will have something that triggers your alarm system and set off the cascade of neuro-chemicals the stress hormones cortisol and adrenaline.

You could be going about your business and feeling fine, when a trigger will send you spiralling into a stressed out heap. Those worthless, 'I can't cope' feelings or overwhelming anger can become all encompassing.

An adult shouting at or smacking a child can trigger me. But even more surprisingly in 2014 a happy event triggered me. You can see this and how I recovered from it on YouTube: - https://www.youtube.com/watch?v=RMdJ54raNwU

N.B. it maybe upsetting for you.

Dealing with your triggers.

For us to understand triggers and how we deal with them we need to revisit the 'stress response' I talked about under Pillar 1 - Clear Conscious Mindset.

We need to know about the role of the Hippocampus and how it deals with new memories and experiences in order to process the flashback, intrusive memories and or nightmare effectively as a result of the trigger.

Remember I explained to you that the Hippocampus along with the Amygdala in the limbic area of your brain controls your reaction to danger/threat.

When your body is flooded with high levels of stress hormones your Hippocampus goes offline and your Amygdala (your primitive brain) remains switched on to danger/threat even if that danger/threat is no longer present.

In order to be able to switch the Hippocampus back on line so that we can process real danger/threat we must understand, deal with and process the triggers so that the flashback, intrusive memory, nightmare does not hold the same power over us.

This book is about making positive lifestyle changes. As you know, I am not a psychotherapist but a Health, Wellness Coach and Mentor. In order to really understand your relationship to your stress, your triggers, intrusive memories, flashbacks, nightmares you may need to seek specialist support therapy... and I'd really recommend you do. It can be life changing.

Please see a list of organisations in the back of this book.

I can also recommend a book that has helped me. It's called *The Warrior Within*, written Christiane Sanderson for the One In Four charity.

This book is about taking small steps in order to help you begin to seek the help you need. For some, lifestyle changes may be enough, for others you will need some form of psychotherapy and I want to help get you there.

Your stressors and how you react to them cannot be undone simply by starting to exercise more. If it were that easy, we'd all be doing it. But exercise, eating well, breathing techniques and just basic self-care can begin to clear your head enough to notice what is going on.

When a trigger occurs, what actually happens to you? And practical steps to help overcome your triggers

As an adult you are always looking after your inner child (the younger you who was abused) It is always there.

When you are overwhelmed - your brain literally shuts down and goes into survival mode. You know those days you have when you can't get started or when something has happened at work or with your family to stress you out and you are in a place of overwhelm you may forget words, you may feel like you are walking through treacle. That's your brain in survival mode and this may trigger your PTS responses.

The best thing you can do in these situations is to bring yourself back to the Here and Now. This is when you talk your mind back to the present from where it has currently 'wandered off to'!

Ask yourself a series of questions:-

Who am I? I'm Sara Miller not Sara Fisher - I'm an adult not the child who is being abused

How old am I? I'm 43 not 8

Where am I? (Bring your attention your current surroundings) I am in my living room in my house not in my childhood home

What is the year? The year is 2016 not 1981

This is a way of you confirming to yourself that you are not in actual danger/under threat.

You are an adult now not the child in an abusive situation. You need to reassure your inner child that everything is okay and that they are safe.

Breathing

One of the best techniques you can learn to help with times of high stress or anxiety, whether caused by an emotional trigger or adrenal fatigue is a technique called 'Belly breathing'.

There's much more on this in the chapters on breathing and exercise but it's worth mentioning here that breathing can really take you out of your stress mode. It's probably the last thing you'd think to do - 'hey I'm really freaked out so I must breathe deeply' - but the most valuable, physical tool you can learn to help you out of a panic and to calm down your PTS response. You need to practice Belly Breathing in times of calm so that you can call upon it in times of need.

Eating

When you are stressed, your body craves sugary carbohydrates. It's a physiological response to the elevated stress hormone cortisol. Your body is demanding more energy to prepare you for the fight/flight response.

Often when we can't speak their truth - in the case of abuse this is very common - we feed our emotions instead. We either self-medicate through food, drugs and or alcohol to calm ourselves down, to make us feel good momentarily. This is often a short term pleasure that causes long term harm.

I learned this first hand whilst writing my first book *Through the eyes of a child*. When chapters were painful to remember I found myself locked in the kitchen comfort eating. It wasn't a conscious act. After a while I started gaining weight and this led into a cycle of guilt and shame and me feeling like a fraud. Everyone knows me as a Health Coach, the person who eats 'clean' and helps others with their fat loss and fitness.

I can honestly tell you that eating nutritionally well has had a major positive impact on my life and continues to do so. Reducing the inflammation in my body has got rid of the stiffness in my hips, the unexplained aches and pains in my body and my mobility has improved.

However at the time of writing the book - my 'stress response' - my subconscious response - to the trauma that was 'playing out' in my brain from me dealing with suppressed thoughts and feelings from the child abuse that I had suffered had the upper hand.

When I realised what was happening I was able to take positive action to change my response. I stopped buying snacks, stopped having them in the house. I told myself that they were for the kids but I was in denial!

When I felt overwhelmed with my thoughts and feelings I chose to react differently. I kept a journal and wrote everything down. My brain was often in the 'past' dealing with issues that no longer had a place in my present. So I would remind myself where I was in the HERE and NOW and talk myself through all the positive things that I had achieved.

I would go for a walk up the garden; looking up to the sky and I would practice my breathing technique 'Belly Breathing' for however long I needed to.

If I was ready I would go back to writing the book if I wasn't ready and needed time out, I would go and do things I enjoy doing which involved me being kind to myself.

It's important for you to identify your stressors and understand how you react to them. Just having an awareness of your behaviours around your stress is a good start.

Start helping yourself. You don't have to be a victim anymore. Start being a survivor and a thriver.

PILLAR 4 - The C.L.E.A.N.E.R™ Living Therapy Programme - ALIGNMENT (POSTURE)

Under this pillar Alignment we are looking at the postures we adopt and how these affect both our mental and physical health.

- Postures we adopt because of the abuse we suffered
- The Foetal position
- The impact of the foetal position on our health
- Signs that your posture maybe affecting your health
- What can we do about it? - Standing Tall
- Optimum Postures - standing, seated and lying

Postures we adopt because of the abuse we suffered

When you have suffered abuse as a child your body wants to curl into a ball, this is a natural reactionary position for you to be in to protect yourself, as an adult this 'curling into a ball' can manifest in other ways.

You don't want to look the abuser in the face.

You don't feel worthy of looking anyone in the face.

As an adult it is difficult to hold eye contact, you think that people can read your mind and see how 'dirty' you really are and how 'unworthy' you are you look down.

You are often fixed into a forward head posture. Head forwards, eyes down which causes migraines, neck pain, and lower back pain.

Imagine your spine. Designed to be held with a natural S shaped curve. For shock absorption and optimal function throughout your body. If your spine is out of alignment this can have a massive impact on your other joints in your body, it can restrict your mobility and cause you pain.

When you have been abused as a child or you struggle with anxiety disorders your muscles are constantly tight. This is the response to your body being constantly in fight /flight mode. Over time tight muscles can pull joints out of their natural alignment and cause uneven wear and tear impacting your mobility and your pain levels.

You don't know how to relax. Your muscles don't know how to relax either.

This can all affect your frame of mind and also your physical health and mobility.

Have you ever considered that the child abuse you suffered could affect your skeletal (skeleton and joints) health and your muscular structure as an adult?

Or that living, wracked with anxiety every day could be affecting your digestion. Not just through stress on the inside but by the way you stand naturally and respond to the things around you daily because of the abuse you have suffered?

I first began to really understand how the child abuse I'd suffered had affected my physical health when I began to investigate the nagging hip pain I had. The constipation, the diarrhoea, the IBS that I suffered.

I had literally spent thousands of pounds going to see experts to find out why my hips were so painful and why my range of movement had become so limited.

To cut a long story short, (you can read the full story on www.christuckmystory.com) after years of tests and scans, experts finally revealed that the ball and socket joints in my hips had virtually fused together. I had early onset osteo-arthritis. I had virtually no cartilage left in my left hip and my right was deteriorating.

It was excruciatingly painful and resulted in a number of operations including a hip replacement in 2015 to get me mobile and moving again.

I believe my hip problems have been caused by years of poor posture and poor nutrition (and malnourishment as a child when I was starved) and then made worse by long hours of studying and having a desk job as an accountant where I sat for long periods of time.

Suddenly I added aerobics to the mix. From years of curling myself into a foetal position to escape the pain of child abuse and to escape being hit physically or mentally I was suddenly expecting my body to cope with jumping up and down, from learning and practicing new routines for hours on end!

The foetal position and its impact on our health

As a growing baby in our mother's womb we adopt the foetal position. Tucking our knees into our chest and curling ourselves into a ball.

In the womb this is a practical position to be in because of the lack of space! But it also makes us feel safe, loved, secure and protected. When we are born it is often advised to wrap a baby up securely in a blanket because they feel safe, loved, secure and protected.

As we grow, we allow our bodies to stretch. We reach out and touch things. We explore the world around us.

When we do something that is harmful or dangerous to ourselves we recoil by running back to the safety of our protector (usually mum, dad or a carer) for a cuddle. We often bury ourselves into our protecting adult. This is our way of making sure we are safe, secure and loved.

Once we have this reassurance that all is okay we feel loved. We feel protected no matter what and off we go again into the world where the cycle often continues.

Each time this happens we are reassured of our protection and it becomes ever easier to spread our wings with less fear.

If your childhood remains happy and you remain healthy and active there would be no reason for you to suffer from poor posture and the ill health that is associated with this.

But what if your childhood did not look like the example above? How could this impact your posture? Your health and wellness?

Sub consciously our brain and our bodies remember the foetal position and what it stands for when we are 'under attack' we revert back to this position of safety, security, love and protection.

If you have suffered physical, mental, emotional and or sexual abuse as a child you will understand this.

This position the 'foetal' position our hip flexors (psoas muscle) can become short and tight overtime.

We can think of your psoas muscle as your body's fight or flight muscle. It's deeply connected to our natural survival instinct. It instantly tightens at moments of danger to either protect you (in a foetal position) or help you run, fuelled by the release of adrenaline.

However, if your psoas is constantly tight, it signals to the body you are in constant danger, which can lead to overworking of the muscular structure and your adrenal glands.

I know that when I suffer emotional stress I can feel my psoas muscles tighten and I feel physical pain in my hips. De-stressing my body can help offset this tightness and the pain I feel

Tight psoas muscles (hip flexors), can cause the lower back to curve pushing out the stomach, causing a number of issues throughout the body. This could be a bad back, sore neck, stiff shoulders, hip dysfunction or even osteoarthritis.

If you undertake high impact exercise or lift heavy weights over a long period of time on an incorrect posture you will cause yourself physical damage. This is precisely what happened to me and what started my fascination with the links between emotional abuse, malnourishment and my posture.

I took my malnourished body which just wanted to be curled in a ball and was used to being sat at a desk and I made it jump. A lot!

I was jumping around to get rid of all my anger but by doing this I was over stretching and working tight muscles into a range of movement they did not want to be in!

My body complained bitterly. I just ignored it because I did not understand the impact of trauma on the brain and the body at the time. I didn't understand the importance of taking care of myself and what I should have done to de-stress my body in the first instance.

If you are suffering pain this is a message to you that something is wrong. Please don't try and push through it like I did. Don't try and just treat the symptoms. Investigate and treat the cause.

Signs that your posture may be affecting your health.

When the psoas muscle works properly, it pulls the abdomen back tucking the tummy in, giving you a strong, flat stomach.

Having an understanding of your posture/your alignment whilst you are standing, sitting, lying will help you address some of your postural issues.

The difficulty with all of this is that when you are in an anxious state or when you have lived with the challenges of child abuse, you simply don't know what standing up tall is anymore.

Yes we know standing up tall is good for us but how do we know what our posture is doing? Most days it feels as though all we can do is survive.

So how do we know that our posture has begun to affect our health?

The most common issues are frequent shoulder problems, headaches, lower back aches, hip pain, stiff joints or breathing difficulties.

We might also notice limits to our range of movement. We cannot lift as high, bend or stretch our limbs like we used too?

It's not all about stretching or standing up tall. Our bodies shut down when they are in pain. They are just in survival mode. They aren't ready to adapt or get stronger. So if you are constantly in pain, over tight or emotionally stressed your body will not work as it should.

This is why we need to begin to deal with our emotional pain in order to see change in our physical selves.

When I am in a relaxed and happy place I notice that my hip joints move better (more range of movement) and there is no pain.

What happens over time?

Over time, chronic tightness can lead to wearing down of the joints. Or if you slouch constantly this can result in a permanent spinal curve and maybe impingement of your nerves.

We might experience a decrease in our brain function or oxygenation of our body.

Poor posture can lead to raised stress levels because of physical stress to the body. Stress isn't just an external thing. It can be brought about from the inside too.

If you are in a permanently hunched over state your digestion could be affected too. The body needs to be more upright in order for peristalsis to occur (the muscle action that eliminates our poo). This could lead to constipation or symptoms often described as irritable bowel syndrome IBS.

Similarly over time our breathing can be affected. If we are permanently bent over we can't breathe through our ribs. Thoracic breathing can't happen easily. So we start breathing in our neck and shoulders. This can lead to poor oxygenation which in turn can lead to our joints, organs and muscles not functioning optimally.

Imagine trying to run a marathon when your body is starved of oxygen. It just won't happen. And this is what you are trying to do if you are permanently hunched and breathing poorly.

What can we do about our posture?
Standing Tall.

The first thing to do is to notice when you are hunching or slouching. We need to begin to have an awareness of what optimal posture looks like for us.

When you are sitting down, have an awareness of how you are sitting. If you are sitting now can you begin to lift up? Get a sense of being tall. You'll start to feel lightness.

Imagine you are trying to give your internal organs a little more space.

When you are standing are you shutting down or are you opening up?

Are you looking ahead?

Try reaching and stretching your arms up over your head. How does that feel?

Imagine an animal or a baby waking. What's the first thing they do? They stretch and reach out. Opening up their bodies. Moving from a curled up, safe position to a completely stretched out position.

When you are beaten, you curl yourself up to be safe. You roll into a ball for protection.

When you encounter a trigger as an adult (and everyone's triggers are different) your sub-conscious doesn't know the difference. You still curl into a tight ball. Even if you don't look like you have, your muscles and joints will have begun to tighten in anticipation. It goes into defence mode.

So here are some challenges for you to help you understand where you may be limiting your physical posture:

Walk down the street looking ahead.

Lie down and pretend to make snow angels (even if there is no snow).

Try to lift your ribs out of your body. Imagine making space for your organs.

Stand up and stretch. Every limb and every digit.

I would highly recommend exercise that helps you stretch and relax before you undertake any form of high impact exercise. Maybe consider getting your posture assessed before you start an activity programme.

Optimum Alignment/Posture whilst standing

Feet - Stand with your feet hip width wide, with the inside if your feet being straight.

Knees - make sure your knees are just straight, not bent or hyper-extended (locked out).

Pelvis - make sure your pelvis is level, lengthen through the small of your back, this will feel like you are slightly tucking your tail bone under. This will stack your spine straight from the base of the lower back.

Shoulders - draw them up to your ears, roll them backwards until the shoulder blades meet in the middle and have a sense of drawing them down your back so that your shoulders are away from your ears.

Neck - lengthen through the back of your neck to the point where your chin is not protruding forwards or on your chest.

Head - your head should be parallel to the ceiling or the sky.

Eyes - your eyes gaze should be straight forward.

When you are in this optimum posture all your joints and muscles will be in alignment. You will experience a sense of lengthening and an opening of your body to the space you're in rather than be shut down and tight fitting into the smallest space possible.

Optimum Alignment/Posture whilst Sitting

- Sit on a chair that is supportive for you
- Feet flat on the floor
- Knees in line with your hips or ever so slightly higher
- Small of the back supported so that your spine stacks up straight
- Shoulder blades pulled back and down
- Arms resting at a height that is comfortable for you

Optimum Alignment/Posture whilst Lying Down

If you lie on your back have a pillow under the back of your head if your head falls backwards and a pillow under the back of your knees so that your lower back does not lift from your mattress.

If you lie on your side stack your shoulders, your hips and your knees. Place a pillow between your knees to prevent pulling on your lower back

Try not to lie on your tummy because this will cause neck pain and lower back pain.

Again like everything optimum posture needs practice. Attending Pilates or Yoga sessions will help you with correcting your alignment/posture and to strengthen your surrounding muscles will help maintain it.

You may need to have your workstation made ergonomically friendly, to prevent injuries such as repetitive strain injury whilst typing.

PILLAR 5 - The C.L.E.A.N.E.R™ Living Therapy Programme - NUTRITION

Under this Pillar we are looking at our Nutrition and fluid intake and their impact on both our mental and physical health. After the introduction we will explore the following:

- Water
- Caffeine
- Chewing
- Digestion
- Vegetables
- Clean Eating v Processed Food and Drinks
- Wheat and Gluten
- Dairy
- Sugar

So here is where we need to stop and stay for a while. We need to quite literally 'digest' this chapter.

The topics above are not in any particular order. Each has their place and each is just as important as each other.

I often say that we need to eat and drink what our bodies NEED not what we WANT. Please bear this in mind as we work through this PILLAR together.

I don't want to bombard you with all the detailed science about what I am about to share with you because it would fill another book! And to be honest there are scientific based books out there in the market place already that I can refer you too. However I will outline the basics and share with you some more detail where necessary and give you practical examples of how you can make changes.

Food and drink so much of how we FEEL can relate back to what we eat and drink and how we eat and drink!

I love this quote from my good friend Cori Withell the Nutcracker remember I shared it with you earlier in the book.

"Our mood affects our food; our food affects our mood".

What Cori meant was our food choices affect our mood and in turn our mood affects our food choices. If you feel good you eat well, if you feel bad you will crave and eat C.R.A.P.

Do you prioritise basic self-care, like preparing and eating food?

We will be exploring what happens to our eating habits and our digestive system when we're stressed or anxious.

I'm going to go into a little more detail here on food but I do want to highlight what are, for me, the three most important things you can do with your diet and eating habits when you are stressed. These three changes will have a significant impact on your health and on the way you feel.

1. **Get off stimulants** - Stimulants like caffeine, alcohol and sugar will stress out the hormonal system more than it already is and make you more anxious.

2. **Cut out processed foods** - Processed foods often contain toxins, which again, can add stress to an already stressed out system.

3. **Chew your food** - Slow down. Take your time. When you chew your food you send the right signals to your body to digest your food.

When you are not looking after yourself you tend to eat quickly. You aren't mindful of what you are eating. After each meal you need to give yourself 10-15 minutes to enable you to eat calmly and digest your food. Invest time, love and energy into your food preparation and enjoyment. Sit and eat your meal mindfully.

What happens when we eat?

Every time we eat there is a hormonal response. When any type of carbohydrate is eaten the body will convert it into simple sugars and a quantity of the hormone insulin is released by the pancreas. The amount released is dependent upon on how high the concentration of the sugar is within our blood.

The converted simple sugars are used for energy for the brain, the muscles, and the rest of the body's cells.

We want to keep the insulin response to our food low. If too much insulin is produced then fat storage will occur.

Insulin 'tells' the cells of the body to absorb sugar (glucose) out of the blood. If too much is produced then fat storage will occur.

If you have the right balance of carbohydrates to meet the energy demands of your body then the insulin produced will be the appropriate amount.

However, if you consume too many sugary/starchy carbohydrates, this will result in an excess of insulin being produced.

This then will encourage fat storage as the excess glucose has to go somewhere, and you will experience unwanted side effects such as weight and fat gain and reduced energy levels.

Sustained high levels of insulin cause us to become insulin resistant. This means our bodies become less sensitive to insulin, our immune systems are low, we become pre-diabetic and our body fat increases.

We can reduce our insulin levels by:-

- Eating good fats such as meat - white meats in the main red meats occasionally preferably organic.
- Supplement with omega 3 - or eat lots of oily fish.
- Reduce starch carbohydrates - Eat low glycaemic responding carbohydrates such as green vegetables.

- Improve your fibre intake from green vegetables - Reduce fructose intake (fruits).
- Reduce alcohol intake (sugar) - increase your antioxidant levels (Green tea is a good source).
- Exercise regularly for short periods (Also reduces prolonged cortisol build up). Building lean muscle mass through exercise can also assist with the distribution of insulin.

Water

We all know water is good for us, yet many of us choose not to drink it. We think it's boring, tasteless or bland. Fizzy drinks or juices seem so much more appealing.

Let's look at **10 good reasons** why water helps you live a better quality of life and what can happen if we don't drink enough:

1. Most of us are dehydrated.

The body needs in excess of two litres (around four pints) of water every day. Consistent long term water consumption helps with detoxifying the body and hydration but it can take several weeks to take effect. Alcoholic drinks, flavoured water or caffeinated drinks can dehydrate us and don't have the same positive cleansing effect as plain old water.

Filtered water is better than tap water since it contains fewer chemicals and more minerals.

2. Dehydration can make you hold on to body fat.

Drinking water is vital to losing fat. You could be eating all the right things but if you aren't drinking enough, your body could hold on to fat reserves.

Your body is designed to remain in a constant state (homeostasis), so if it isn't fully hydrated it could cut back on certain functions, rationing water supply to vital functions like brain and circulatory health.

3. Dehydration can lead to joint pain.

Cartilage in your joints is mainly made of water. During movement these joint surfaces glide over each other and some cells become worn. The body produces new cells to replace damaged or worn ones. Water is required to transport nutrients to help maintain cell repair in your joints. Without enough water the joint compartments could become closer together and result in increased friction, wear and tear.

Muscle cramps are also a common sign or side effect of dehydration.

4. Your blood needs water.

Blood may be thicker than water but it's around 83% water. Less water circulating around your body means less blood. This can lead to reduced blood pressure, headaches, dizziness and even a rapid heartbeat since the heart needs to pump faster to make up for having less blood.

5. Dehydration and histamine.

If the body doesn't get enough water, it protects itself by rationing the water it does get. Vital organs like the liver, kidneys and glands are prioritised, as well as muscles, bones and skin (one of the first signs of dehydration is dry skin).

During long periods of dehydration your body will focus on brain function, reducing water supply to muscles, joints and digestive organs. This is when you could start to become toxic.

This process is largely managed by a neuro-transmitter called histamine. Chronic dehydration can cause histamine to become over active, which can cause symptoms of other disorders like asthma, constipation, rheumatoid arthritis, migraines, depression, muscle and joint pain.

This is what happened to me. As a child my water intake was restricted because I wet the bed. I wasn't allowed to drink after 5pm until the next morning. (The reason I wet the bed I was scared and anxious most of the time!)

My body got used to the water famine but I suffered as a result. My digestive system was severely sluggish resulting in chronic constipation - I went to No.2 every 7 to 10 days. The constant straining lead to bleeding and an anal prolapse. I had two operations to fix the damage.

For some of my childhood food was restricted or non existent; as an adolescent and young adult I used to eat untold amounts of fruit and was too lazy to prepare vegetables. I ate low fat products and margarine and plenty of pasta because I thought this was all good for me!

Unfortunately this created an acidic and toxic environment within my body. The lack of water, my poor nutrition, my poor posture and over-exercising eroded the health of my hip joint.

I will explain more on this as we explore nutrition in more detail and the other PILLARS. Remember all the PILLARS are interlinked and one impacts the other.

Once I realised what my problem was I made sure I upped my water intake and I have never had a problem since.

6. Check your urine

A simple way to check your hydration levels is to look at your urine. A pale straw colour and odourless is ideal. Dark and smelly means you need to drink more. If you only urinate once or twice per day you are very dehydrated. Some vitamins can make your pee very yellow which is different to the dehydrated state of urine.

Some people find adding a tiny pinch of good quality sea salt to their water helps your body to retain water and remain better hydrated and this will also boost you adrenal glands.

7. Chlorine in water

Chlorine in tap water can block the absorption of iodine in the body. Fluoride is added to UK drinking water to protect children's teeth. There is a lot of research online to show that tap water is not healthy for us. Please check it out and make your own mind up about this. I have a Brita filter in my kettle and I have a filter on my water bottle. You can also buy a water filtration system for your kitchen if you choose to.

8. Water helps regulate body temperature.

Insufficient water in your body means your body cannot efficiently cool itself. This could lead to heat stroke or heat exhaustion. The opposite is also true. You may not be able to warm up or you could feel chronically cold.

People can live for over a month without food but less than a week without water.

9. Water is brain food.

Water helps you stay fresh, alert, wise and on the ball. Hydration helps us to detoxify the body. Toxins can cause brain fog.

Hydration is such a basic tool on the road to wellness but often overlooked and can cause ill-health as we have seen above.

10. Action for you:

Aim to drink 2-3 litres of clean fresh water per day. This will be dependent on your body weight. It is recommended that we drink 1 litre per every 50lbs of bodyweight

I weigh 9st 7lbs = 9*14lb + 7 = 126lbs / 50lbs = 2.66 litres.

If you know you don't drink enough water and you find it hard to do start by drinking

500ml by 9am

500ml by 12pm

500ml by 3pm

500ml by 6pm

500ml by 9pm

You will need to up your quantities if you are heavier.

Carry a bottle around with you all day long, keep sipping from it and refilling it.

If your mouth is dry you are dehydrated.

N.B. Do not 'binge' on water. This is drinking too much water too quickly. This can lead you to dilute the salts in your body - Hyponatremia and you can become very ill quickly.

Remember if you have caffeine or alcohol to you will need to offset this with even more water.

Caffeine

Most of us love a cup of coffee. Coffee shops are popular and a great place to catch up with friends or to meet. But have you ever stopped to consider how coffee affects you? Did you know it affects your hormones for example?

Let's start with instant coffee. Unfortunately, regardless of brand (or cost) instant coffee is highly processed and a lot of chemicals are used to create it. So in addition to the caffeine you have a fairly high risk of extra toxins to process.

All coffee and black tea (unless it's de-caffeinated) contains caffeine, which can be problematic if you are already a stressed out person. Stress can show itself as pressure from work or home, or nutritional stress if you have a poor diet.

Caffeine can interfere with adrenal function (the small glands sitting on top of the kidneys). Your adrenal glands are there to help your body cope with stresses. Your energy, endurance and life all depend on them functioning. Excessive caffeine consumption (which can differ from person to person) can contribute to adrenal fatigue.

Caffeine can also increase oxidation in cells which could lead to premature aging.

Caffeine can also stay in your blood stream for up to nine hours if you are sensitive to it. So this could keep you awake even if you last drank caffeine in the early afternoon.

Like all things, some people are just more sensitive to caffeine or the bi-products of processing coffee than others. Some people may be affected by the oils produced by roasting coffee, whilst others could react to the chemicals used to create de-caffeinated tea and coffee.

It is just better avoided. And whilst a coffee detox is challenging, it will be well worth the effort. Focus instead on nourishing your body, especially if you are sensitive to caffeine. A coffee detox can last between 24 and 48 hours and you can feel pretty rough as your liver processes toxins - this can cause headaches. Stay well hydrated or consider a sauna to sweat out the toxins.

If you really want to go back to coffee after a detox, stick to organic beans or coffee you grind yourself, this way you'll get the caffeine without the chemicals.

Remember caffeine robs your body of minerals like magnesium, calcium, B vitamins, Vitamin C and antioxidants. So if you must drink coffee, make sure you have a great diet or supplements to keep your vitamin levels up.

Vegetables

Why are vegetables important for your health and well-being?

Vegetables are packed with vitamins, minerals and lots of trace elements that help to keep us healthy.

Cruciferous vegetables like broccoli, kale, cabbage and cauliflower are high in vitamin C. They are also high in anti estrogenic compounds like indole-3-carbinol, which stimulate detoxification (gets rid of toxins) and help prevent the build-up of fat around the belly (estrogenic fat). They also are anti-inflammatory and have cancer-fighting properties.

Vegetables are so important to good health that the World Health Organisation (WHO) recommend we eat **between 9 and 11 portions of vegetables per day.** (http://www.who.int/dietphysicalactivity/publications/f&v_promotion_initiative_report.pdf?) This is more than double the 5-a-day that the UK government recommends. Most of society associate their 5 a day with eating fruit not vegetables. Eating too much fruit can cause high insulin spikes and overtime weight gain. There is some evidence to suggest the nutrients found in our fruits and vegetables are on the decline due to changes in farming practices and nutrient deficient soil. If it's not in the soil, it's not in the vegetables we eat.

A 2001 study published in the Journal of Complimentary Medicine (Worthington et al, 2001) showed that US and UK Government statistics show a decline in trace minerals in fruits and vegetables by up to 76% in a 51-year period between 1940 and 1991.

This evidence suggests we need to eat more vegetables to prevent the chance of developing nutrient deficiencies, which are linked to many common illnesses.

We all know that we need to get more vegetables into our diets, the trouble is, and not everyone (especially children) is a fan of these super foods.

For optimum health you need to be eating a balance of good protein, carbohydrates (carbs) and fats on a daily basis and at every meal.

Vegetables are carbohydrates and fall into two categories:

Good Carbohydrates (carbs)

Fibrous (non-starchy carbs) - have lots of fibre and water in comparison to the starch/sugar they contain. The fibre/water and low level sugar balance out hormones, staves off cravings, making you less hungry and keeps your energy levels stable. These include vegetables and less sweet fruits (berries, apples, pears, and grapefruit).

Non-fibrous (starchy/sugary carbs) - include everything else. Beans, legumes, lentils, sweet potato, brown pasta, brown rice, potatoes, oats.

Bad Carbs

These may contain one or all of the following: trans fats, sugar, artificial flavourings and preservatives. They stress your digestive system by causing inflammation in your body. Bad carbs include bread, biscuits, cereals, cakes, crisps, processed foods. All of which will cause weight gain if eaten consistently and persistently over time.

The main source of the carbohydrates (carbs) you eat should be fibrous.

Fibrous carbs, including many green vegetables, typically have very low carbohydrate content. Their inherent high fibre brings about a very moderate insulin response, thus making them an ideal fat loss food. Research shows that the higher fibre content of most vegetables will delay carbohydrate absorption, favourably modifying the glucose response. Dark green vegetables usually have a large antioxidant content as well (not as great as dark fruits, but still a sizeable amount).

The best sources of fibrous carbs include:

- Kale • Broccoli • Lettuce • Cabbage • Cauliflower • Mushrooms • Green beans • Onions • Asparagus • Cucumber • Spinach • All Forms of Peppers • Courgettes • Cauliflower

N.B. Sweet Potatoes - are a good source of protein, fibre, beta carotene, vitamin C, folate and calcium, sweet potatoes are a nutritious and tasty family food. Contrary to their name, sweet potatoes are not botanically a potato, but rather a root. Though white potatoes contain much more niacin, sweet potatoes are overall more nutritious: They are lower in carbohydrates and higher in fibre, beta carotene, folic acid, and calcium. Like potatoes, sweet potatoes are best stored in a cool, dry pantry. If refrigerated, they lose their taste.

I have already shared with you under the topic of water what happened to me when I was dehydrated, getting too much sugar from fruit and not eating enough vegetables.

Now I make sure I have something 'green' at every meal.

Here is a list of top hydrating vegetables

Courgette: With 95 percent water by weight, Courgette is one of the most hydrating vegetables you can eat. A healthy serving has less than 25 calories and is an excellent source of folate, potassium, and vitamins A and C.

Bell Peppers: Colourful bell peppers are 92 percent water, yet they're still rich sources of some of the best nutrients available, including vitamin C, thiamine, vitamin B6, beta carotene, and folic acid.

Romaine Lettuce: It may have slightly less water than iceberg lettuce, but romaine contains 3 times more folate, 6 times more vitamin C, and 8 times the beta-carotene. Use it as a sturdy base for more substantial salads

Carrots: Carrots contain about 87 percent water and more of the powerful antioxidant beta-carotene than any other vegetable or fruit. Studies have found that compounds in carrots help protect again skin, lung and oral cavity cancers.

Raw Broccoli: Vitamin C, fibre, calcium, and few calories. Need we say more? (Just in case: It's composed of 91 percent water, too!)

Celery: Crunchy celery is 96 percent water, but it also provides a combination of mineral salts, amino acids and vitamins that research shows may hydrate your body twice as effectively as a glass of water.

Raw Spinach: At seven calories per cup, hydrating spinach is undeniably a great food to fill up on when you want to lose weight. One cup provides more than 50 percent of your daily vitamin A needs, as well as being high in protein and vitamin C.

Tomatoes: Tomatoes are composed of about 95 percent water. That means that along with signature sweetness comes enough moisture to cut back on (or take the place of) higher-calorie condiments on your sandwich.

Cucumber: The flesh of cucumbers is primarily composed of water but also contains vitamin C and caffeic acid, both of which help soothe skin irritations and reduce swelling—which is why cucumbers are often used to help swollen eyes and sunburn.

Mixed Greens Salad: Most lettuce greens contain 94 percent water, making it a low-energy density food. In other words, you'll feel fuller on fewer calories and lose weight faster.

Butternut Squash: This sweet and nutty squash is 88 percent water. A cup of cooked butternut squash also boasts over 400 percent of your Daily Value for vitamin A—a key nutrient for eye health—as well as healthy doses of vitamin C, potassium and manganese.

Here are my Top 14 Tips on how to sneak more vegetables into your daily nutrition:

1. Skewer vegetables like cherry tomatoes, carrot slices, mushrooms, aubergine, onion, squash or sweet potatoes, for tasty shish kebabs.

2. Make homemade guacamole and use chopped vegetables like carrots and celery instead of crisps or breadsticks.

3. Replace bread with lettuce wraps for sandwiches or burgers.

4. Replace toast soldiers with vegetables for dipping with your boiled eggs.

5. Make vegetable salsa and use it in place of creamed sauces on meats, fish, and chicken.

6. When eating out, order starters that feature vegetables. Ask your waiter to swap the potatoes and instead bring two side orders of steamed vegetables with your meal.

7. Cut sweet potatoes and parsnips into half-inch strips and roast them in coconut oil for a tasty alternative to French fries.

8. Once a week, have a meal salad for dinner, such as Cajun-salmon Caesar salad or grilled-chicken spinach salad with mandarin oranges.

9. Make a simple avocado salad for lunch.
10. Mix steamed swede and/or carrots into mashed potatoes.
11. Roast chunks of carrots, sweet potato, celery, and onion in coconut oil, with a little sea salt and pepper, and a few sprigs of fresh rosemary. Roast at 425 degrees for 30 minutes. Great with a Sunday roast.
12. Roast cherry tomatoes, red onions and bell peppers, courgettes, garlic and basil in a little coconut oil. Awesome with a nice piece of steak.
13. Make a stir fry using spinach, broccoli, and baby sweet corn. Great with baked salmon
14. Make your own vegetable soups

Make your own vegetable stock

Boil up all manner of vegetables, potatoes, celery, carrots, turnip, swede etc., and drain. Store the liquid in ice cube trays to use directly in recipes. When needing meat stock, add in the bones/carcass to the veggies. Don't forget to season!

I hope the information above gives you inspiration and motivation to improve the uptake of your greens.

I love juicy smoothies and I use my Nutribullet regularly to give my body the nutrients it needs. I often have a greens juice in the morning and add a small handful of fruit to my smoothie just to sweeten it. Make sure you don't put too much fruit in your smoothie otherwise you are just giving your body a sugar bomb which will give you a huge insulin spike which will be followed by a crash.

Chewing

Lots of people get uncomfortable flatulence, gas and bloating on a weekly and sometimes even a daily basis.

We think this is normal but often gas and bloating are symptoms of something not quite right in the diet, the gastrointestinal system, or both.

These are our top five reasons you could benefit from chewing your food slowly:

- **Reduces bloating**

Often there's just a lack of digestive capacity. Enzyme production is low, acid production is sluggish, bile production is inadequate. These factors mean food doesn't get broken down well. These large, unbroken molecules that haven't been broken down properly hit the small intestine, creating gas and bloating there.

- **Reduced acid reflux**

If you also have acid reflux, or take antacids or acid blocking drugs, you probably have reduced digestive capacity.

- **Increase awareness**

Stop multi-tasking. Eating whilst doing lots of other 'stuff' will distract you from what you have eaten and feelings of fullness. Watching television, answering emails, working on the computer, on Facebook, on Twitter, basically ignoring the food on your plate whilst eating is a recipe for indigestion and hunger! Before you are aware of it, the food has gone, your plate is empty, and you are still hungry. It's possible you'll reach for more food. You may not even notice you've eaten anything else.

- **Relax**

The next time you make the effort to shop, cook and eat - take the time to savour the flavours, the spices, and the textures, the colours of the food you've just prepared and put all that effort into. After all it takes about 20 minutes for you to actually feel the effects of being full. So instead of spending five minutes to eat your dinner (because you are in a rush to do something) next time, slow down, take time off from the world. Give your digestive system a chance.

- **Drop fat**

If you pay attention to your food you will find you eat less. You will feel fuller.

Digestion improves when you chew your food slowly. Digestion actually starts in your mouth, not your gut. The gut should receive properly chewed food!

By chewing your food, you will allow it to be digested fully and all the nutrients contained within that food will be absorbed.

Unchewed food causes 'stresses on the digestive system and you know all about stress by now!

Digestion

Have you ever wondered how your digestive system works? Apart from the obvious fact that we just eat and expect our gut to do the rest?

We believe our digestive systems will just cope with anything we put in. That it will just digest and take out the exact minerals it needs to keep bones and muscles healthy and blood topped up with the vitamins and minerals it needs to keep us 100% healthy and protein, fats and carbs it needs to keep our brains and bodies functioning.

We only really stop to think when something goes wrong. Something like a bloated belly, gas, constipation or acid reflux. These are often caused by poor digestion and usually curable by great digestion!

So exactly how does digestion work?

Digestion starts in our brain. We see and smell food which sends signals to our brains. Our mouths water, saliva increases and digestion begins in your mouth.

Chewing slowly helps food to be broken down to release nutrients required for a healthy constitution. But many of us eat too quickly without savouring or acknowledging our food.

On entering the stomach, it's mixed with enzymes an HCl (more on that later). Here it is broken down into amino acids to be absorbed into the small intestine.

Food eaten too quickly, which hasn't absorbed well, can give the small intestine too much work to do. It may struggle to absorb food molecules, which can lead to immune problems in the system, parasites or fungi in the gut.

The small intestine is about 25 feet long. Along each section, you will find little receptor sites that absorb foods. From here, the pancreas enzymes and bile from the liver are released. So if everything is working well, the digested food moves into the large Intestine.

At this point however if there's a problem, undigested particles of food can pass through the gut wall and into the system, like a foreign particle entering the blood stream, which can create immune responses.

Digested food moves onwards to the large intestine which is five - six feet long. The colon

Absorbs some of the vitamins and minerals present and recycles any water for the body. So if you are dehydrated, water is extracted and what's left can become compacted. This is a great reason to drink more water! - To help with the elimination of your body's food waste.

When Digestion Goes Wrong.

If your digestion is affected by food choices and isn't coping there are THREE common issues:

1. **Insufficient HCl (Hydrochloric Acid)**

Insufficient HCl increases your risk of belly bloating after you have eaten, or increased wind! It kills the unfriendly bacteria in the gut - parasites and germs. You can take supplements like Swanson's Hydrochloric Acid and Pepsin.

Include red onions, garlic and fermented foods like Sauerkraut into your diet since these have more sulphur the same is true for red onions. I love red onions and add them to dishes I cook or add them raw to my salads...

Make it simple and it's a habit that will stay with you.

2. Dehydration

Insufficient water can lead to constipation and a colon back log.

The body needs water. When it's dehydrated it squeezes water from the faeces in the colon which can cause constipation.

Toxicity from the back log can go into the bloodstream.

Constipation can cause back pain. The large intestine is five - six feet long, three inches in diameter and is situated at your lower back, the descending colon gets backed up and your back can feel it.

This is why I always ask clients about food and water intake when I'm treating them for back issues.

3. Heartburn

Heartburn isn't always a sign of excess stomach acid. It can be a sign that you are dehydrated.

Gastro-Oesophageal Reflux Disease (GERD), the scientific name for heartburn or acid indigestion is NOT caused by excess acid production but too little.

With insufficient acid, the gut can't digest the food properly to extract minerals and vitamins.

In order to produce stomach acid (Hydrochloric acid) you need sodium chloride, or salt.

So it's important to keep some salt in your diet. Some regular table salt, which has had all of the nutrients and minerals taken out, isn't good for you but you could replace salt in your diet for Himalayan sea salt. Grind your own salt in a salt cellar to make sure you are eating the best quality salt possible.

When the stomach gets protein for digestion, your body starts to produce acid. When the acid doesn't arrive it keeps sending for the acid, this is when heartburn can start. It's like a car engine, if you have ever had trouble starting a car and overdo it by pumping the accelerator too much you flood the engine, the body works in a similar way. With no Hydrochloric Acid it asks for more. If it doesn't get it, you can end up with GERD.

Over the counter tablets could suppress acid further and make it worse. It's worth tackling your diet and hydration before reaching for medicine. As with most health niggles, it's usually your body giving you a sign that something isn't quite right.

Digestion is really important for the production of serotonin (our happy hormone).

4. HTP - your happy amino acid - Serotonin.

One of your body's essential amino acids (found in proteins and food) is HTP.

This amino acid assists in the production of the chemical serotonin, the body's feel good chemical.

HTP is used to treat depression, insomnia and migraines.

You may have a serotonin deficiency if you suffer from low moods or lack of sleep.

80% of serotonin production is in the gut.

By looking at your nutrition and your digestion, you can help yourself to increase the absorption of minerals and vitamins it needs; increasing serotonin production In the gut.

Not all forms of depression can be solved by increasing serotonin levels in the gut but for some of us, this is worth trying.

Once you know and understand more about your body's processes and digestion, you are better equipped to try dietary tweaks to see if they help you, before you resort to medication such as anti-depressants from the GP to address your symptoms.

Your Vitamin D levels will affect the release of serotonin. Serotonin is a natural combat of cortisol (your stress hormone). For many people vitamin D levels are too low.

Getting out into the sun for 30mins per day can restore Vitamin D levels but most people leave for work in the dark, stay indoors all day and arrive home in the dark.

Always talk with your GP before making drastic changes to your diet but adding in good, healthy nutritious foods and reducing processed foods (cheap ingredients and cheap salt for example) is always a good start.

Clean Eating v processed food and drinks

Clean eating has been around for years. It's just another way of saying, 'don't eat rubbish'.

The health of your mind and body begins with your cells. Your body is made up of trillions of cells. Each of these cells has its own function. In order to do its job effectively it needs the right fuel. Each cell needs to receive the correct quality and quantity of nutrients to maintain their structure (what they are made up of) and to perform their function (the job that they have to perform).

When you eat food or fuel that your body recognises - in other words food that it can break down and absorb and use as fuel - you feel good because your mind and body are functioning as they should.

You're full of energy. You're alert and focused. You will have strong bones, teeth, hair, skin and nails.

The fuels you need are called **nutrients**.

Macro nutrients are protein, good fats and carbohydrates so this is your chicken, meat, fish, nuts and seeds and vegetables

Micro nutrients are the minerals and vitamins which we generally get from vegetables, fruits and legumes.

You also need lots of clean fresh water to process your food and to keep you alive.

When you eat differently to this; when you eat C.R.A.P. you will not feel your best. You may become lethargic and you may suffer from migraines, aches and pains and mood swings.

- Caffeine
- Refined and sugary food
- Alcohol
- Processed Foods

Unfortunately over the decades consuming C.R.A.P. on a daily basis has become the normal, modern day diet. I call C.R.A.P non-foods because they are non-nutritional - they do not add any nutritional benefit to your body.

There's very little nutrition in processed foods (in spite of the clever marketing).

That's why foods are often fortified with vitamins.

Many processed foods also contain artificial colours and flavours, sugar and artificial sweeteners. Sometimes these are added to increase shelf life or just to make them taste better or to keep your taste buds addicted to processed foods.

Some people believe they are eating healthily because they are eating everything in moderation but moderation could mean three chocolate bars per day as an average for some people.

A better guideline is two to three treats per week as part of a healthy eating plan.

Are you close to that?

When you eat C.R.A.P foods your body does not recognise them. It treats them as toxic, and your body can't break these non-foods down. These non-foods are hard to absorb and are not good sources of fuel.

So what happens to these non-nutritional foods?

Toxic foods are shuttled away to your adipose (fat) tissue where they attract water.

Your body wants to dilute the toxicity within the cells and expel the toxins from your body. But as you bombard your body with more and more non-foods your liver becomes overwhelmed and can't cope. Your liver's main function is detoxification, if it's overloaded your fat cells fill up and then you grow some more, they fill up and the cycle continues.

Over time your continued eating of non-foods will make you gain weight and swell up from water retention.

Not everyone finds every non-food toxic to their system. If the quantities you eat and drink do not overload your system you'll cope for a while, but it will eventually manifest itself in some way. You may not be the size and shape you want to be because of your stress, lifestyle choices, eating patterns and activity levels. All of which will impact your hormones, your size and shape and how you feel about yourself.

It can be a vicious cycle - let's look at this cycle.

An event or trigger happens in your life, causing you stress. This can trigger the fight or flight mechanism which makes you crave carbohydrates like chocolate and crisps, alcohol, drugs, whatever your default coping strategy is.

Often once you start you cannot stop. You become trapped in the cycle.

In order to break the cycle, you need to understand what is happening to you and the importance of eating nutritious food.

Nutritious food keeps your hormones in harmony. If one hormone is out of whack the hormonal cascade kicks in and your physical, mental and emotional health can and often will suffer.

When you have suffered abuse you are already dealing with many mental, emotional and physical challenges. You do not need the added stress of poor nutrition.

I do understand that if you don't feel good about yourself or if you think you don't deserve it, your food and fluid choices may not be the best! I have been there too on many occasions.

It's vital that your nutrition is excellent and that you stay well hydrated. You need to focus more on your diet than others in order to cope with the trauma and stress of abuse. The same is true if you are someone who suffers with anxiety disorders. Your nutrition is paramount to your health and ability to cope with life's ups and downs.

Clean Eating goes back to basics and removes all of the foods that your body treats as toxic. These foods are replaced with only wholesome, preferably organic and nutritionally supportive foods.

By eliminating certain foods for a little while you will give your body a chance to 'catch up' by getting rid of stored up toxins and excess body fat, whilst feeding your body the nutritious (not boring!) food that it needs.

Here's an overview to foods that may be toxic for your body:

Wheat and Gluten

Wheat and gluten are often used interchangeably, they are closely related but they are not the same.

Gluten is a protein found in wheat, barley and rye. All wheat contains gluten but gluten is found in other sources too.

Wheat has been hybridised by man over many years. It is very different to the ancient grain we originally ate. This was done to make wheat easier to make bread with and easier to harvest.

We are no longer eating the wheat how nature intended It to be, man has manipulated it too much.

Wheat is extremely hard for humans to digest. In addition to the grain we often have to digest pesticides, vermicides and fungicides too. It is then bleached to make flour products.

The effects of wheat and gluten on our mental and physical health

When gluten (contained in wheat) is ingested, it goes through the gut and has a massive impact on our brain chemistry.

Gluten is used in cooking to bind food. It is used in a growing number of products and forms a build-up of plaque liked film on your brain and has been linked to cognitive diseases such as Alzheimer's, Parkinson's and cancers....

- It is not designed for human consumption.
- It is highly addictive and causes food cravings
- It is highly inflammatory - it causes bloating, affects your skin, causes arthritis
- It increases your waistline - you will have 'wheat belly'

Many people eat way too much wheat and gluten on a daily basis:

- Toast for breakfast;
- Sandwiches for lunch;
- Cookies, biscuits and cakes as snacks; and
- Pasta for dinner.

This can cause the digestive system to become overloaded.

This was me! I have already discussed the health problems I had before I started the C.L.E.A.N.E.R.™Living programme.

What can we use instead?

Spelt is a good alternative. It's more like our original wheat grain. Grains like spelt and kamut have a higher protein content and higher profile of amino acids, fats, vitamins and minerals than wheat and are easier to digest unless you are very sensitive to gluten. If you are gluten intolerant then you need to search out gluten free products. Please steer clear of the FREE FROM foods in the supermarkets; these contain many e numbers and other ingredients that will affect you.

If you have coeliac disease please speak to a specialist.

Now I always try and find healthier alternatives to non-foods which affect my digestive system, my moods and my pain levels.

I do not eat pasta anymore I use courgette ribbons as my spaghetti and sauté this in coconut oil.

I have bread, crackers, cakes, biscuits occasionally - usually more so on special occasions like birthdays, Christmas and holidays.

When you remove wheat and especially gluten from your diet you may feel unwell for a few days but this will soon pass. In a few days your brain chemistry will begin to rewire and change, you will feel sharper, become more focused, your memory and other symptoms will improve.

Remember you can be wheat intolerant but still have gluten in other products but if you are gluten intolerant you cannot have wheat or any other product that contains gluten.

Top Tip - Cook from scratch! If you cook from scratch you will know what ingredients are going into your food, you will not have to worry about wheat or gluten.

Dairy

Do you remember being told to always drink your milk, it's important for your calcium levels and strong bones! When I was young it was compulsory to have a bottle of milk at school at break time. To be honest even though I now know that milk is not good for me back then I really looked forward to that bottle of milk due to the lack of food available at home!

There is a lot of research around whether or not dairy products are good for us and like everything you need to be your own food detective and smart consumer. When consuming dairy products how do they make you feel? Do you suffer any adverse reactions?

Many of us are allergic to dairy products but we just do not make the connection with the symptoms we are suffering to the foods we have eaten. When I started to learn about what I ate and drank and the effects on my health and wellness it was mind boggling but also life changing.

Non-organic dairy produce contains hormones which could potentially disrupt the balance of our reproductive hormones. It's estimated there are over 60 hormones in an average glass of non-organic milk.

Today's milk is also heat treated so much of the goodness is lost.

After around the age of two, we no longer produce the enzyme 'lactase' which enables us to effectively break down milk proteins.

Dairy refers to anything made from animal milk like cheese and yogurt.

Milk powder is also included in many cakes and processed foods which can make them harder to digest.

The effects of dairy on our mental and physical health

Dairy products do contain calcium but unfortunately, most of it is in a form we cannot digest well.

- It is not designed for human consumption. Though cow's milk may be the perfect food for baby cows, it's not necessarily the best thing for adult human beings
- Dairy is inflammatory for many people causing :-
    1. increased mucus production,
    2. sinus congestion,
    3. respiratory problems,
    4. digestive symptoms (such as gas, bloating, diarrhoea, or constipation) and skin problems like eczema, dermatitis and psoriasis

What can we use instead?

Did you know that you get 75% more calcium from spinach than you do from milk!

Good non-dairy sources of calcium include tinned sardines, nuts, seeds, pulses and green leafy vegetables.

If you're going to drink cow's milk, then it's best to drink milk from grass-fed, organic, non-hormone treated cows

You can also use alternatives to cow's milk like coconut milk or almond milk. Please do not use Soy milk, this is highly processed.

Our bones stop growing by our early 20's so we can keep our bones strong through weight bearing exercise. As we get older this is very important to prevent osteoporosis. I have a lady called Hazel in my 60+ class who suffered from osteopenia and she has her bone density checked regularly. Since coming to the Forever Young Fitness class and taking part in movement and weight bearing exercise her bone density has improved drastically and she is no longer at risk.

It is never too late to make lifestyle changes that will benefit both your mental and physical health.

Sugar

There are a million reasons why we should avoid sugar. For years it was thought or we were lead to believe that eating fat made us sick and obese. The truth is sugar is the main culprit!

Sugar contributes to Type 2 diabetes, heart disease, depression, high blood pressure, hyperactivity, mood swings, fatigue, skin issues like Rosacea and Eczema, premature ageing, kidney issues, and weight gain...

Sugar affects your immune system which can make you more susceptible to colds and flu.

Sugar is more fattening than fat.

Sugar takes on different guises in our diet including alcohol, dextrose, glucose, high fructose corn syrup, agave syrup, honey and fruit.

If you eat more fruit than green vegetables you will benefit from switching this around.

Fruit can ferment in the gut and lead to IBS issues and insulin spikes which leave you craving more sugar.

Fruit like berries, apples, pears, pineapples and bananas are great but try to keep to two portions per day. If your gut and skin can't cope with that perhaps reduce it even further.

Reducing fruit for breakfast and replacing it with protein and greens can make a big difference if you are an IBS sufferer or have skin concerns like Eczema.

Here is a list of the top hydrating fruits:-

Watermelon

A 2009 study at the University of Aberdeen Medical School (http://www.abdn.ac.uk/) found that the combination of salts, minerals and natural sugars in some fruits and vegetables can actually hydrate people more effectively than water or even sports drinks. Watermelon was on top of the list, thanks to its 92 percent water content and essential rehydration salts calcium, magnesium, potassium and sodium.

Pear

Beyond their sweet, refreshing taste, one medium pear contains 6 grams of dietary fibre, or 24 percent of the daily recommended value. Plus, the type of fibre found in pears (soluble fibre) helps you feel full for a longer period of time, which means it can help you lose weight.

Apple

You've heard it before: An apple a day keeps the doctor away. But this juicy superfood has also been linked to lower cholesterol levels, weight loss and preventing a host of chronic health woes—cardiovascular disease, asthma, diabetes, and even certain cancers.

Grapefruit

According to researchers at Scripps Clinic in California, the chemical properties of grapefruit lower insulin levels and help control appetite, which can lead to weight loss. Try adding half a grapefruit to your breakfast or drink a glass of freshly squeezed grapefruit juice any time of day.

Strawberries

Make a habit of snacking on these hydrating berries (they're 92 percent water). Studies show that people who eat one serving of strawberries per day tend to have higher blood levels of the B vitamin folate, which helps keep arteries clear. Go ahead and splurge for organic. According to a 2010 study from Washington State University, organic strawberries are more nutritious and flavourful than those that are grown through chemical-laden farming.

Raspberries

Raspberries deliver more fibre (8 grams per cup) than any other commonly consumed berry. Plus, they're packed with ellagic acid, a powerful antioxidant that is thought to help prevent and fight cancer (particularly skin, breast, lung, bladder and oesophagus).

Wild Blueberries

Is there anything blueberries can't do? Studies have linked this superfruit to everything from cancer prevention and better heart health, to anti-aging and improved eyesight.

It's very hard to break a sugar habit. Especially if you were given sweet treats as a child. Try to focus on the benefits of eating less sugar rather than the sweet hit you are missing.

Sugar will not benefit your good gut flora either. Cutting it back and replacing with green vegetables, fermented foods (sauerkraut for example), red onions, garlic and sulphur will help your digestion.

Comfort food isn't always comforting when the results of eating comfort food time and time again make you sick and tired, not just physically but mentally.

Clean foods go a long way to improve your health.

The healthier you are, the less fat your body holds onto.

Here are a few of the benefits we hear about in the fitness industry from people who chose healthy lifestyle over a processed life

- Stabalisation of blood sugars, hormones and moods
- More energy to run around after the kids, run for the bus, walk up and down the stairs, walk around the shops, walk on the beach without getting out of breath
- Ability to maintain the body shape and size you want
- Reduced pressure on your joints so your back, your hips, your knees and feet will feel less pain
- Improved sleep patterns - better quality of sleep and longer duration of sleep
- Improved circulation
- Heart and lungs functioning more efficiently
- Liver working more effectively because it is less burdened at dealing with toxins
- Bright eyes, clear skin
- Flatter stomach - no bloating
- Improved digestion - no constipation, diarrhoea, flatulence
- Alert and focused - no mental fog.

"Your food affects your mood; your mood affects your food"
Cori Withell - The Nutcracker

PILLAR 6 - The C.L.E.A.N.E.R™ Living Therapy Programme - EXERCISE

Under this Pillar we are looking at our Exercise and its impact on both our mental and physical health.

Exercise

I love exercise. In many respects I owe my life to it.

Exercise has saved me from my darkest moments. It's got me out of the pits.

Time and time again when a trigger hits me and I spiral down, it's exercise that's able to pull me back up again.

Exercise is one of the many jobs' I have. I'm part accountant, part activist, part fitness and lifestyle coach. So it affords me the freedom to live my life my way. I can take time off when I want to, but I hardly do!

I'm always helping victims and survivors in some way.

1. Peer 2 Peer Support
2. Campaigning
3. Writing articles, newsletters, books and hosting weekly Facebook live broadcasts to discuss topics surrounding child abuse.
4. Speaking at conferences and workshops raising awareness of the impact of child abuse on the individual and trying to get more dedicated allocated funding for specialist support services specifically for adult survivors of non-recent abuse.
5. More recently in the last 12 months setting up the charity SOB and working at IICSA as a consultant.

As a survivor myself the above work impacts me on a daily basis. I'm not complaining I have chosen my path but I need an outlet to counterbalance the impact of my work.

Exercise for me is this outlet. I hear you ask…is Chris addicted to exercise?

No I'm not I just know how important it is to my health and wellness - my mental and physical health. Over the years I have changed the type of exercise I do, I cross train and rest.

Exercise lets me meet and help people. Through my work as a lifestyle coach I attract and connect with some of the most incredible people. Through fitness and nutrition I've literally seen lives transformed including my own.

So I'm a massive fan of exercise. In fact one of the major inspirations for this book is knowing that exercise, nutrition and an understanding of child abuse and mental health disorders can start the road to recovery.

I do however also understand that when you are at the lowest point of depression or anxiety, even leaving the house can feel like a step too far. I know that because I've been there too.

Why is exercise so good for survivors of abuse or those living with anxiety?

One of the reasons exercise is so good for survivors of abuse is that it allows you to get some control back over your life. Even if you are afraid to leave the house, making progress with regular exercise at home can begin to build your confidence and the endorphins released when you exercise will make you feel good and more positive. - If you begin to succeed in this area of your life, you could begin to use this behaviour in other areas. Like seeking professional counselling or letting go of self-harming behaviours.

By exercising, you are doing something for yourself. Showing yourself that you are worth taking time out for, that you are worth looking after. It doesn't need to be expensive or showy and it doesn't even need to be an hour at the gym. Just 15 minutes every day could be enough to start to make a change, to begin to make you feel better about yourself.

Every positive change you make and adopt will have a ripple effect on all other areas of your life.

What exercise is the best for you?

Any type of exercise that you enjoy and that you can be consistent with is the best exercise for you.

- This might be walking up and down your stairs at home.
- This might be attending a Zumba class with your friend
- This might be walking the school run instead of driving it
- This might be running a Couch to 5K or a Marathon!
- Taking part in a HiiT class (high intensity, interval training) or weight training
- Swimming or cycling
- Pilates, Yoga, Tai chi or meditation

When you are stressed or going through trauma, non-impact exercise like Yoga or Pilates is a great way to centre yourself and calm your mind and body. It might feel like the last thing you want to do if your brain is going at lightning speed but it can make you feel so much better.

Tai chi, swimming, Pilates, yoga or meditation are all great ways of helping your body to unwind. We discussed the fight or flight response in earlier chapters this is how your body switches to 'fight or flight' mode. Holistic, low impact forms of exercise can actually help your body revert back to the parasympathetic nervous system - or the relaxed and happy state. So please bear this in mind when you are choosing an exercise activity suitable for you, for your current state of being and any injuries that you may have.

Of course there are exceptions to the rule, which is where understanding your own responses to stress and exercise are so important, or working with a coach. When I got into exercise on my road to recovery, I found aerobics was an effective way of getting rid of negative emotions.

I was able to process my anger through exercise whilst getting an endorphin release. As I have got older, continuous high impact exercise is not good for my joints so I keep my HiiT sessions short and adapt them to suit my needs and I do more Pilates, meditation and belly breathing.

Above all it's about finding something you enjoy. Something you can stick to. A Yoga or Pilates retreat or an active holiday might be a good place to start. We run Breaking the Cycle™ Retreats to help individuals experience everything we have talked about in this book.

Learning a new skill can also be really helpful. Learning tennis, learning to dance, taking part in a choir can be a fantastic way of relaxing. These types of skilled sports need you to be in the moment. They can take you away from your thoughts as you focus on what you are learning or doing.

Buying a pet can have a massive positive impact on your mental and physical health. I have a Springer Spaniel called Duffy and no matter what the weather I have to walk her. When I'm stressed or need to speak to someone and no one is around I can stroke her and talk to her. This has a calming effect on me.

Pets are not demanding and give unconditional love (most of them!) I know many victims and survivors have pets especially cats or dogs for this very reason.

Getting started

For some people just the thought of leaving the house is too much. So for absolute beginners or for those of you who are suffering symptoms that are keeping you housebound I'd recommend you buying a basic pedometer and count the amount of steps you do on a daily basis.

Try and do 10,000 steps per day. You may have to build up to this. Make sure you record your progress so that you can see your achievement.

If walking is too much for you, you can do simple mobility and movement sitting in a chair.

It does not matter what your current state of health and mobility is - there is always room for improvement.

Joining a group

Are you ready to join a group, a class or a gym? In the early days having a sense of community when you work out is really important. Not only will it hold you accountable and ensure you get out of the house (having to get out for a class at a specific time is actually easier to do than getting out for a vague appointment - everyone knows you have to go) but meeting up with a group makes it so much easier to get motivated.

Above all you need some sort of plan, even if it's progressing to doing 10,000 steps a day. A class instructor will have the plan for you as would a Personal Trainer but if you are going it alone schedule your workout days in your diary and aim for progress, not perfection!

The science of exercise and wellness

There is a magic to exercise which is actually scientifically based. Here are just a few examples of how exercise can impact your body:

Have you ever wondered why your fit friends always have so much energy? Exercise increases the production of mitochondria [KELLY et al, 2006].

Mitochondria are like the body's own battery or energy cells. So exercise can give you more energy.

Gentle exercise, like yoga, pilates or walking can help manage stress. This is now measurable through heart rate variability (HRV). HRV is an excellent tool to measure early signs of stress. This technology is now available on lots of smart phone apps.

Heart rate elevation for 20 minutes increases blood flow to the heart and the strength of the heart wall.

Exercise which is fun produces dopamine, a happy hormone. Some intense exercise also produces endorphins which make you feel good. This can improve your emotional health.

It's important that you exercise at the level you need at this point in your journey of recovery. It will help you discharge the stress hormones in your body. Exercise was and is the way I control my anger and gets rid of any negative energy I may have.

Over-exercise

No chapter on exercise and mental health would be complete without mentioning over exercise. It is an actual thing.

When I worked at the Priory, where I learned a lot about addiction, I also learned that exercise addiction was very common. One addictive behaviour can easily be swapped for another, and addicts often do swap one coping behaviour with another unless they deal with the root cause of their problem.

Exercise addiction is usually identifiable by a person doing a lot of exercise! Doh!! You don't say! We're talking 2-3 hours every day. That person would usually feel anxious if they weren't able to exercise. Or they'd feel guilty over skipping a workout. Like any addiction they will do anything to do it - to get their fix.

If you are coming off drugs or alcohol, where you've been used to numbing your feelings with drugs, the highs you get from exercise could replace that numbing. This is why often it's the low impact, breathing focused exercise activity which is so good for survivors of abuse or for those struggling with addiction.

Long periods of exercise especially high impact exercise can cause further stress to the body and increase cortisol production. Remember this is our stress hormone!

Exercise is literally a stress on the body - which used in moderation, can help your body adapt over time by getting fitter or stronger. Too much high impact or long periods of exercise could make cortisol production or adrenal fatigue worse.

Fitness online

I have recorded some exercise videos that may help you get started.

Copy the links into your browser and let's get started!

Remember you are doing this at your own risk and if you are in any doubt whether you should be taking part in exercise please check with your GP first.

1. **Make sure you complete the warm up before you do every short workout**

BTC Warm Up - https://youtu.be/HFt2tyFWXRw

2. **Choose and complete a workout**

BTC Simply 12 Challenge -   https://youtu.be/Pq8NKJ3kvt4

BTC Leg Blast Challenge -   https://youtu.be/ezl3Vjs65AY

BTC Abs Blast Challenge -   https://youtu.be/1BtGdise2IA

BTC Triple Challenge - https://youtu.be/vz57PG9bx2U

BTC 100 Challenge -   https://youtu.be/11bc1u3-2s0

3. **Make sure you complete the post workout stretch after every exercise session.**

BTC Post Workout Stretch - https://youtu.be/v3Dm1fiOXoU

4. Here is a MOBILITY workout video for you which is gentle!

https://youtu.be/GHENAmWxNXQ?list=PLZRCpMKHU-yJyjXeyEhTzVBE6690ljnpb

You can either stand or sit to do this Mobility workout.

There are more workouts on my YouTube channel that you can access if you wish https://www.youtube.com/user/ctsfitness

PILLAR 7 - The C.L.E.A.N.E.R™ Living Therapy Programme - REST and REGENERATION

Under this Pillar we are looking at Rest and Regeneration and their impact on both our mental and physical health.

Have you ever found yourself tired but struggling to get to sleep at bed time?

Perhaps you lay there, thinking or worrying.

Eventually you fall asleep but you might wake in the night and immediately begin to worry again, which prevents you from falling asleep.

When it's time to wake, you want to go to sleep again!

One of the first things to be affected by emotional stress is sleep. The cycle of tired-sleep-worry is common in those suffering from stress, especially if you are a victim or survivor of abuse who is suffering from trauma related stress responses such as triggers, intrusive memories, flashbacks or nightmares

Sleep and rest needs to be equally as important as nutrition and exercise. We recover as we sleep; no sleep, no recovery, no ability to put your effort into the exercise, your work or anything else.

If you can get your sleep cycle RIGHT everything CAN fall into place!!

How do you feel when you have a bad night's sleep? (Poor sleep or a few hours?)

Lack of sleep or poor sleep, even if you are getting enough, can cause many problems including:-

- Headaches,
- Poor recovery from exercise,
- Neck pain,

- Lack of focus on work tasks
- Moodiness
- Craving for C.R.A.P (caffeine, refined sugars, alcohol and processed foods)

Sleep and the Circadian Rhythm

- If you can get your sleep cycle right (circadian cycle) then everything can fall into place.
- The circadian cycle is a natural physiological cycle of about 24hrs that persists even in the absence of external cues - light being a big factor here.
- If light stimulates your skin or eyes your brain and hormonal system will think its morning - the normal and automatic reaction to this is the release of cortisol. This is not good when we are trying to de-stress our body!

Circadian Rhythm Cycle - Morning

A natural cycle our bodies should follow is in line with the sun:

- Wake at about 6am - our bodies have acceleration in activity physically and mentally between 6am and 9am - best time to exercise and do paperwork!
- Cortisol levels are high in the morning and they should decrease over the course of the day to allow you to be mentally and physically alert.
- Drink liquorice tea

Circadian Rhythm Cycle - Daytime

- As cortisol levels naturally drop off (unless stressed)
- The release of growth hormones increases.
- The release of growth hormone allows fat cell release and increased fat burning potential.

Circadian Rhythm Cycle - Evening

- Wind down and go to sleep around 10/10.30pm
- Physical repair occurs between 10pm and 2am - so if you are not getting to bed until 1am there's not a lot of time to recover physically before the next element.
- Mental repair kicks in from 2am to 6am.
- This then has a knock on effect of less ability to function properly the next day.

What happens if we don't get to bed early enough?

- Stress (cortisol) levels stay raised for longer,
- reducing the ability for the growth hormone release,
- Therefore cutting down your potential fat burning time but also your physical and mental repair!

So although we look at nutrition and exercise, we have to look at sleep not just for rest, repair but for fat burning.

We must respect the circadian rhythm to achieve our goals for health and wellness.

So what can disrupt these cycles?

- Stimulants! Caffeine, sugar, tobacco. These are the most commonly used things to 'get energy' - a pick me up

- BUT these trigger a release of CORTISOL again!

- Caffeine from strong coffee can stay in the body for 6 hours at a higher level then another 6 hours at a lower level, so drinking caffeine after lunch can mean you still have a stimulant causing cortisol release way past the 10pm repair stage - you are battling with yourself at this point!

Stimulants and the Cortisol Cycle

- Sugar causes a rise in insulin - causing it to store blood sugar, then there is an overcompensation response, so blood sugar goes low and the body then goes into emergency mode releasing - guess what??? Cortisol!! To trigger a release of glycogen from the liver bringing sugar levels back up.

- Before the body has a chance to correct itself people feel low blood sugar effects and eat more or have more caffeine thus further releasing Cortisol

- So don't take on the sugar, don't get caught up in the cycle and then don't release the cortisol which would further effect the circadian rhythm - point here is if you have this level of sugar after lunch it will act like the caffeine - so no stimulants after lunch time on a regular basis.

- You need rest and recovery in an aim to reduce body fat but maintain strong muscle tissue (the stuff that burns more fat!!)

- The body can bounce back after odd occurrences of stress but long term can have serious implications to long term health.

How to improve poor sleep

There are general ways to help you cope with poor sleep cycles However If you are suffering from trauma related stress responses you can either:-

- Read a self-help book like *The Warrior Within*
- Visit your GP and get referred to a Trauma Specialist for treatment such as EMDR
- Or pay for your own treatment with a Specialist Support Service

Here are the top tips I put together with Lifestyle and Movement Coach and NLP Practitioner Mel Collie http://melcollie.com/

1. **Turn off all technology one hour before bed time.** That's computers and mobile phones. Don't check the phone for messages and if you use it as an alarm - set it an hour before bed. If you use a digital alarm clock, turn it away from your bed. Even a small amount of light can disturb your sleep. Make sure your room is dark. Invest in some black out curtains.

2. **Use the hour before bed to unwind.** Have a hot bath; dim the lights or light candles. Read a novel that takes you away from your reality into a fantasy world.

3. **Have a mug of Tulsi or Chamomile tea an hour before bed.** This will help you to relax more. Tulsi is an Indian herb that can help reduce your stress levels and can also help with hormone balance.

4. **Aim to be in bed by 10pm at least five times a week.** If you'd usually go to bed at mid-night, start slowly reducing the time you are awake before midnight. So start at 11.30 and gradually bring it forwards. Your body will quickly adjust. Your body and your hormones love sleep before midnight. It's the recovery sleep time.

5. **Stay hydrated.** This means skipping wine, tea or coffee. These are all stimulants and may keep you awake or wake you in the night. Well hydrated bodies sleep better since they are better able to repair and renew cells.

6. **Invest in some stress reducing herbs like Ashwagandha and Rhodiola.** These herbs can actually help you to adapt to stress better by reducing the over activity. These herbs are known as adaptogenic. Ashwagandha helps your body to achieve balance and aids coping with stress and anxiety - which in turn helps sleep. Rhodiola helps with depression, improves mood and can reduce fatigue - this is better taken earlier in the day and Ashwagandha, later in the day to prepare for bed.

7. **Increase your magnesium levels.** Many people, especially stressed out people are deficient in magnesium. All our cells need magnesium.

   Tablets, sprays or Epsom Salts in the bath are a wonderful relaxant and a great way to increase magnesium levels.

   Magnesium tablets can be beneficial too but not in the form of magnesium oxide since this will be excreted. Look for an 'ate' like sulphate, citrate or stearate since these will be absorbed by a healthy digestive system. Take magnesium tablets 90 minutes before bed

   Other Vitamin and Mineral supplements - you may need supplement with a B Complex Vitamin, Vitamin C and Zinc. Most health food shops can help and advise you with this.

8. **Tackle your airways.** As you reach middle age and beyond, your throat becomes narrower and the muscle tone in your throat decreases. Men have narrower air passages than women and are more likely to snore.

   A narrow throat, a cleft palate, enlarged adenoids, and other physical attributes that contribute to snoring are often hereditary.

   Nasal and sinus problems can also contribute to restricted airways, making inhalation difficult and creating a vacuum in the throat. This is what can lead to snoring.

   Being overweight or de-conditioned can also add to snoring. Fatty tissue and poor muscle tone contribute to snoring.

Alcohol, smoking and medications which act as muscle relaxants can also increase snoring.

Sleeping on your back can also cause the flesh in your throat to relax and block your airway.

9. **Improve your liver function.** During the night your liver is working hard to try to detoxify. Your liver metabolises anything that has gone into your body which shouldn't be there from sugars and MSG to chemicals on food.

   The liver does most of its work between 1 and 3am - so if you wake between those hours you would benefit from a full liver cleanse.

10. **Stimulate tryptophan.** Tryptophan will help you sleep. Eating a banana an hour before bed can help this.

Your plan of action

Now that you have read the book and have a greater understanding of the 7 PILLARS of the Breaking the Cycle™ C.L.E.A.N.E.R.™ Living Therapy Programme.

It is time to take stock of where you are.

And compare this to where you need to be in order to improve your mindset, your stress levels, your nutrition and fluid intake, your life style choices and behaviours.

Now remember if it all feels too daunting for you, you need to break it down into smaller steps. It has taken me years to get to where I am now and I still have setbacks.

Understanding the process of your own recovery and healing is unique to you.

To restore control, to take charge of your life and your future takes time, patience, stamina, hope and commitment.

The Warrior Within book by Christiane Sanderson for the One in Four Charity talks about using a metaphor that reflects your recovery.

For me this is the Breaking the Cycle™ C.L.E.A.N.E.R.™ Living Therapy Programme because it encompasses many factors that you need for your recovery and growth.

- It's all about putting yourself first,
- It's all about investing in yourself,
- It's all about self-discipline, self-reflection and self-monitoring
- It's about best practice for you which is nurturing, loving and caring for you!

But ultimately it's about regaining control, taking charge for yourself and your future.

- It's about identifying your inner strengths and weaknesses
- Building your support network
- Regaining control over you and what you want from your life
- Having a sense of purpose - setting yourself some goals to achieve.

It's important that you pace yourself and avoid rushing otherwise you could trigger your alarm system and set off the 'stress response'.

- Pick one PILLAR at a time and work on the advice under that PILLAR until you have mastered it and then move onto the next PILLAR that you feel you could achieve at this moment in time.
- Remember you may go backwards at times but this is all part of your healing journey.
- Remember taking small positive steps in one area of your life will have a ripple effect on all areas of your life.

You must record your achievements and reward yourself along the way. Valuing your achievements and take pleasure in them. Every step you take towards your journey of healing and recovery counts!

Keep a Promise/Achievement Jar!

Coming out of survivor mode

This means that you are gradually balancing negative feelings and experiences with positive ones. Balance will open up opportunities to make meaningful choices rather than you being controlled by negative thoughts, feelings or abuse experiences.

When you are in survival mode and feeling low you do not have the energy or the mental space to notice positive things in your life.

Counterbalancing traumatic experiences

To aid recovery you need to counterbalance traumatic experiences

Reclaiming pleasure

- By reintroducing pleasure into your life,
- Living in the present
- Having renewed energy for life
- Reclaiming yourself

Re-claiming pleasure is part of your self-care.

During your childhood you may have been denied certain things. Reclaiming them now as an adult is often empowering and liberating.

1. If you were silenced as a child - as an adult choose to sing, shout and scream!
2. Were you starved as a child like me? - as an adult know that you can eat when you want, what you want. Cook good nutritional meals, eat slowly and enjoy your food. Remember you don't have to binge eat or eat your food quickly. You can have treats when you choose to but remember their impact on your health!
3. Do you find it hard to trust people? As an adult you can choose who you let into your life or choose to trust an animal instead!
4. Were you surrounded by negative people growing up and find yourself in the same situation as an adult? Choose your friends and colleagues wisely.

> *"You are the average of the five people you spend the most time with."*
> *- Jim Rohn*

If you hang out with positive people they will lift you up, if you hang out with negative people they will drag you down!

So for me my pleasure list would look like this:

- Daily activity - mix of walking, HiiT, Pilates, Meditation
- Listening to music
- Reading fictional books
- Writing
- Public speaking
- Watching comedy
- Eating out
- Cinema with my daughter
- Cooking with my son
- Regular holidays

What does your reclaiming pleasure list look like?

Living in the present

The more you can do this the more at peace you will be in your life. Practicing being grateful for what you have and what you are currently working on often opens more opportunities for you.

Living in the past can make you stuck in the past. With all the negative feelings and emotions that come with that.

We cannot change the past but we can change the way we react to it. We can learn lessons and use those lessons to make us happy today and build the future that we really want.

Living in the present means being happy and enjoying the moment whatever that happens to be.

Find a way to give back and find the beauty in something that is happening around you.

> ***Remember the past, plan for the future, but live for today, because yesterday is gone and tomorrow may never come.***
> ***- Unknown***

Renewed Energy

When you are not looking backwards all the time, when you are achieving, helping others, giving back, enjoying the moment, and surrounding yourself with positive people you will have a sense of renewed energy to live your life to the full.

Reclaiming Yourself

Reclaiming yourself to live a healthier and happier life and to fulfil your potential is your ultimate goal.

REMEMBER

I Believe in You! /   You Are Worthy! / Go and Break The Cycle™.

I AM ME, NOTHING MORE, NOTHING LESS.

Be the best version of you; you can be.

Health and Happiness

Chris xx

Contact details

Facebook: www.facebook.com/CT.WWHF

Twitter: twitter.com/ChrisTuck_WWHF

LinkedIn: www.linkedin.com/in/ChrisTuckSOB

For access to the Breaking the Cycle™ Secret Facebook Group, contact me via sobbtc@outlook.com or on my social media links above.

Want to attend a workshop? Check out http://www.survivorsofabuse.org.uk

Through the eyes of a child by Chris Tuck - available from Amazon

Parenting without Tears by Chris Tuck - available from Amazon

Thank you

To all the victims and survivors out there, I would like applaud you for your strength and courage. I wish each and everyone one of you health and happiness. I want to thank you for buying and/or downloading this book. I would love to hear your feedback please email me, Chris, at sobbtc@outlook.com.

I have managed to write this book because of my experiences of child abuse and neglect and because of the wealth of knowledge and expertise I have gained from the courses I have attended, the books I have read and the people I have worked with and spent time with.

I would like to personally thank:-

Emma Kenny - TV psychologist, presenter, writer and expert commentator for writing the foreword for this book - http://ekenny.co.uk/

Chris Day, the corporate sponsor for S.O.B http://www.filamentpublishing.com/

Diane Sealey. Diane is a friend, trustee and PR Expert for S.O.B - http://fibrepr.co.uk/

Andrew Crawford. Andrew is a friend, trustee and accountant for S.O.B - http://www.fitnessindustryaccountants.com/

Tracy Weight for helping S.O.B gain charity status.

Mel Collie Lifestyle and Movement Coach. Mel co-created the Breaking the Cycle™ 8 Week Online Programme with me and I have used some of the resources in this book - http://melcollie.com/

Karen Laing, my ghost writer - http://www.karenlisalaing.com/

Dax Moy. Dax has been both a friend and mentor to me. The activities within this book I completed with Dax as part of his coaching programme. I also studied posture and nutrition with Dax - http://www.daxmoy.com/

Rachel Holmes. Rachel has been both a friend and mentor. Rachel is the creator of Kick Start Fat Loss. I studied nutrition and Pilates with Rachel. I am one of Rachel's many KSFL Business Owner's nationwide - http://www.kickstartfatloss.net/

Jacqueline Hooton, my friend and No.1 supporter. Jacqueline is the creator of http://www.wifeevents.com/

Christianne Wolff for offering me invaluable advice. Christianne is the creator of www.thebodyrescueplan.com/

I would like to also thank and make a special mention of **Paul Mort**, **Phil Richard**s, the **KSFL Team**, all the **Fitpros** who have raised much needed funds for S.O.B, and finally **Kim Meyler Vincent**, **Elly Moore** and **Charley Tuck** for their help with editing the book.

Resources

Telephone Helplines

The organisations listed below offer someone to talk to, advice and sometimes face to face counselling.

Childline

Children can phone **0800 1111** (free) or write to Freepost NATN1111, London, E16BR if they are in trouble or are being abused. Also for parents, children, abusers and professionals **0808 800 5000 (24 hour help line)**

Family Matters

Counselling service for children and adult survivors of sexual abuse and rape.
13 Wrotham Road, Gravesend, Kent DA11 0PA.
Telephone 01474 536 661
Monday to Friday 9am to 5pm.
Helpline 01474 537 392

Rape and Sexual Abuse Support System

For women and men, staffed by trained female volunteers.
Helpline 01483 546400 (Women).
Helpline 01483 568000 (Men).
Sunday to Friday 7:30pm to 9:30pm

NAPAC (National Association of People Abused in Childhood)

NAPAC is a registered charity base in the UK, providing support and information for people abused in childhood.
42 Curtain Road, London, EC2A 3NH
Support line 0800 085 3330
www.napac.org.uk

Survivors UK

For male survivors of rape and sexual abuse.
Helpline 0845 122 1201
Monday and Tuesday 7pm to 9:30pm
Thursday 12pm to 2:30pm
www.survivorsuk.org/

SAFE: Supporting Survivors of Satanic Abuse

Helpline for survivors of ritual and satanic abuse. Offers Counselling, listening, advice and referrals.
Telephone 01722 410889
Wednesday 6 30pm to 8:30pm
Thursday 7pm to 9pm
PO Box 1557, Salisbury SP1 2TP

Samaritans
24-hour listening and befriending service for the lonely, suicidal or depressed.
Telephone 08457 90 90 90

Victims Support line
Telephone 0845 30 30 900
Monday to Friday 9am to 5pm
Weekends 9am to 7pm
Bank holidays 9am to 5pm

Preventing Abuse

Phone one of the helplines listed previously or contact the following agencies if you suspect a child is being abused or is at risk of abuse, or you know of an abuser who has any contact with children.

Police
Many districts now have a special police unit that works with sexual abuse. Phone your local police station and ask to speak to the officer who deals with sexual abuse.

Social Services
Phone your local office and ask for the Child Protection Officer or the Duty Officer. If you are abusing Children or have urges to abuse children phone the NSPCC or contact Social Services or the police.

Therapy/Counselling and Support

One in Four
One in Four offers a voice to and support for people who have experienced sexual abuse and sexual violence.
219 Bromley Road, Bellingham, Catford SE6 2PG
Telephone 020 8697 21 12
Email admin@oneinfour.org.uk
www.oneinfour.org.uk

Respond
Respond works with children and adults with learning disabilities who have experienced abuse or trauma, as well as those who have abused others, through psychotherapy, advocacy, campaigning and other support. Respond also aims to prevent abuse by providing training, consultancy and research.
32 Stephenson Way, London, NW1 2HD
Telephone 020 7383 0700
Email admin@respond.org.uk
http://www.respond.org.uk/

MOSAC

Mosac is a voluntary organisation supporting all non-abusing parents and carers whose children have been sexually abused. We provide various types of support services and information for parents, carers and professionals dealing with child sexual abuse.
MOSAC, C/O The Deborah Ubee Trust, 20 Egerton Dr, London SE10 8JS
Telephone 020 8293 9990
Email enquiries@mosac.org.uk
www.mosac.org.uk/
National Free Helpline: 0800 980 1958

Other

Citizens Advice Bureau (part of the overall grouping Citizens Advice)

Can direct you to local groups who can help. Find the number of your nearest office in your phone book. **www.citizensadvice.org.uk**

EMDR (Eye Movement Desensitisation and Reprocessing)
For information about EMDR and help to find an accredited therapist in the UK.
www.emdrassociation.org.uk

MIND
Offers individual counselling and group work.
Information Helpline
0845 7660163
Monday to Friday 9am to 5pm
Email info@mind.org.uk

Relate
Can help with relationship difficulties and sexual problems. Provides couple counselling, face to face or by phone.
Premier House, Carolina Court, Lakeside, Doncaster, South Yorkshire DN4 5RA
Telephone 0300 100 1234
Email enquiries@relate.org.uk

Beacon Foundation
Services for survivors of satanic/ritualistic abuse and their carers, and support for professionals.
3 Grosvenor Avenue, Rhyl, Clywd LL18 4HA
Helpline 01745 343600 (helpline)
Weekdays 10am-4pm

The Survivors Trust
A national umbrella agency for 130 specialist voluntary sector agencies providing a range of counselling, therapeutic and support.
www.thesurvivorstrust.org

National Association of Christian Survivors of Sexual Abuse
An international organisation run by survivors for survivors.
c/o 38 Syndenham Villas Road, Cheltenham, Gloucestershire GL52 6DZ
napac.org.uk

SNAP (Survivors Network for those abused by Priests)
www.snapnetwork.org

Action for Children
Provides national network of child sexual abuse treatment centres- providing support and counselling for children and their families. Adult survivors also.
Chesham House, Church Lane, Berkhamstead, Herts HP4 2AX
Telephone 0300 123 21 12
www.actionforchildren.org.uk

S.O.B Survivors Of aBuse
Hosts workshops for victims and survivors to aid their recovery from childhood trauma.
www.survivorsofabuse.org.uk

Special Agencies

CICA (Criminal Injuries Compensation Authority)
Telephone 0800 - 358-3601
www.cica.gov.uk

Bolt Burdon Kemp specialise in compensation claims for survivors of child abuse.
**Contact Dino Nocivelli 0207-288-4887 or Mobile 07557 115028
Email dinonocivelli@
boltburdonkemp.co.uk**
http://www.boltburdonkemp.co.uk/child-abuse/

This is not an exhaustive list. Please GOOGLE other services in your area.

If you are in crisis, please go and see your G.P or your local A+E Dept.